Painted Clay

For my Father

First published in Great Britain in 2001
A & C Black (Publishers) Ltd
35 Bedford Row, London WC1R 4JH

Copyright © 2000 Paul Scott

A CIP catalogue record for this book is available from the British Library

ISBN 0-7136-4754-X

Front cover illustration: *The Scott Collection: Commission for the Royal Victoria Infirmary, Newcastle. River panel.*
Painted underglaze on porcelain with screen printed inglaze decals, 1.80m x 0.65m, Paul Scott, 1998.
Photograph by Keith Paisley.

Back cover illustration: *The Scott Collection: Commission for the Royal Victoria Infirmary, Newcastle. Leazes panel.*
Painted underglaze on porcelain with screen printed inglaze decals, 1.80m x 1.30m, Paul Scott, 1998.
Photograph by Keith Paisley.

Title page illustration: *The Scott Collection, Cumbrian Blue(s) 2000:*
A Millennium Willow for Sellafield or *Plutonium is Forever (well 24 Millenia Anyway).*
Inglaze screen print in cobalt blue on bone china platter with gold rim, 32cm dia., Paul Scott, 2000.

Designed by Dorothy Moir

Printed in Hong Kong by
Wing King Tong Co. Ltd

PAINTED CLAY

Graphic Arts and the Ceramic Surface

PAUL SCOTT

A & C Black • London

Thanks to:

Anne and Ellen.
My editor Linda Lambert.
AN Publications.

Paul and Audrey Kettle, Maria Geszler, Nina Lobanov Rostovsky,
Charlie Krafft, Léopold Foulem, Richard Milette, Neal French,
Hans Van Lemmen, Maureen Michaelson, Su Lupasco Washington,
Marianne de Trey, Maria Sulyok, Maruta Raude.
Terry Bennett, Rachel Mann, Andrew Morris.

To all the artists who have lent images, provided information and spent
their time answering my questions, by telephone, letter, fax and email.

All the Museums, Art Galleries and Private Galleries that have been
instrumental in providing images and information, in particular to:
Velta Raudzepa at the Decorative Applied Art Museum in Riga,
Dr Irmela Franzke at the Badisches Landesmuseum Karlsruhe,
Suzann Greenaway at Prime Gallery Toronto,
Sharon Gater and Lynn Miller at the Wedgwood Museum,
Lisa Beth Robinson at the John Michael Kohler Arts Centre,
Gretchen Adkins at the Garth Clark Gallery,
Deborah Smith and Sherrie Joseph at the Art Gallery of New South Wales,
Winnie Tyrrell at the Burrell Collection,
Elizabeth Conran and Howard Coutts at the Bowes Museum,
Jósef Sárkány of the Janus Pannonius Múzeum Pécs,
Miranda Benion at the Royal Academy,
Harry Frost at the Museum of Worcester Porcelain,
Elizabeth Jackson at the Percival David Foundation,
Julia Poole and Diane Hudson at The Fitzwilliam Museum,
Walter Maciel at the Rena Bransten Gallery,
Julie Clements and Janet Partridge at the Ashmolean Museum.

Contents

Preface

A number of years ago, there were no books that examined the processes of printing and ceramics in any digestible literary form, and I approached Linda Lambert at publishers A&C Black. She took the gamble, commissioned a publication, and in 1994, the small handbook *Ceramics and Print* was published. Shunned by some as focusing on an area of only 'very specialist interest', the little handbook took off. Two years on, I was curating the touring exhibition which grew out of it: 'Hot Off the Press'. This exhibition began to look at the reasons . . . why print? What were the differences between printed ceramics and traditional studio pottery?

By then, there was no shortage of suitable work for the show, yet I found myself having to omit exhibits that I would have liked to include because they were painted, not printed, and it was then that the idea for this book began to take shape.

Introduction

Looking at the various publications on the history of ceramics, it is clear that what we have been fed for many years is a particular version of ceramic history. It crystallised for me when one day I heard a well-known potter describing the painting on Italian maiolica as lovely *'decoration'*. What we have had is the history of pottery. Here *form* and *function* are the key words and it is they that dominate the thinking and philosophies of those who have written and taught. So any treatment of the ceramic surface is about the use of glazes, smoking, burnishing, the effects of the wood or salt kiln, and any painting or drawing is, critically, simply defined as decoration. The focus has been self-referential; lots about pottery, objects, domesticity, about clay, glaze and firing . . . not the other things that are out there in the rest of the world.

The notable exceptions are those academics who have made it their business to study the ceramics of a particular time or genre. Thus we have incredibly detailed accounts of the varying periods of Greek vase painting, Islamic tiles, of Italian maiolica, or Soviet Propaganda ware. In some of these cases the terminology used to describe the ceramic surface is more enlightened than the vocabulary of mainstream studio pottery. But even here, there is a sense that painted ceramics is understudied and undervalued: Timothy Wilson in the introduction to his book on the Fortnum collection of maiolica at the Ashmolean Museum in Oxford observed: 'Nor is maiolica often studied alongside other forms of Renaissance painting. Fortnum's wonderful objects are a standing reproach to the fact that the "industrial arts" have still not established their proper place in the mainstream of university art history in Britain.'

In addition, the physical material a work is made from usually signifies a relative value within the visual arts. Artist Conrad Atkinson writes: 'In terms of hegemony of artforms, certain are privileged over others. This hegemony has been severely shaken and possibly stirred over the past few decades. The collapse of the avant-garde and the dissolution of modernism have both contributed to this. Whereas a stroll around the Burrell Collection[1] would suggest that at the top of the hegemony in the 14th and 15th century embroidery by anonymous aristocratic ladies was important and certainly above the as yet underdeveloped easel painting . . . a look at the last three decades would suggest that at least with the thinking classes the notion of easel painting as the prime artform has received a severe dent with the advent of performance/installation/the women's movement/minority visibility and the attempt to categorise certain activities as craft and others as art . . . The debate continues.'[2][*]

There is physical evidence of the debate, and a shifting of values. In recent years the Museum Het Kruithuis in the Netherlands has pursued a policy of collecting the ceramics of 20th-century fine artists, and has published books examining the phenomena. The Picasso ceramics show at the Royal Academy in London in 1998 also indicated a general resurgent interest in the ceramics produced by fine artists.

In spite of this, there is still a lingering sense that fine artist ceramics are not in the same league as their paintings or sculptures. Writing about the 1998 Picasso show in *The Guardian*, Adrian Searle observed that: 'According to Norman Rosenthal, exhibition secretary at the Academy, there has been resistance to the very idea of this show . . . Others raised their eyebrows – the ceramics? This is Picasso for kids, Picasso retreating into play in the post-war years. Picasso going into production and turning himself into kitsch, then.'

---

[1] Burrell Collection: Gift of Paintings sculpture, stained glass, tapestries, ceramics, furniture, silver, metalwork, and objects d'art donated to the City of Glasgow by Sir William Burrell (wealthy Glasgow Ship owner with life-long passion for art collecting), now displayed in the award winning museum of the same name in Glasgow, Scotland.

[2] Conrad Atkinson, *The Plate Show Catalogue*, Collins Gallery, Glasgow 1999.

[*] See also Paul Greenhalgh's essay 'The History of Craft', in *The Culture of Craft*, ed. Peter Dormer, M.V.P. 1997.

Above Pablo Picasso: *Face* , 17/1/65, 42.5 cm. Photo: Images Modernes.

Today (with lots of books on 'pottery decoration') there has still been no serious attempt to plot a discernible path through history, illuminating key moments or times in the graphic development of the ceramic surface, and I have found nothing that specifically looks at the contemporary state of painting, drawing and printmaking in ceramics. Why is this and what are the reasons that ceramic painting and graphics appear to have been undervalued both by the fine art community, and (at the same time) by those in the world of studio ceramics?

The answers are complex and lie, to a large extent, in history. Perceptions of the word 'art' are, at the end of the 20th century, in an almost constant state of flux, but from the Renaissance until the early part of the 20th century, painting, sculpture and architecture were considered to be the *'fine arts'*. Ceramics were at best peripheral to these, and have been variously defined as belonging to the *applied arts* ('a name given to a type of art that is intended to be the opposite of fine art because it is useful rather than sim-

ply evidence of artistic activity') or the decorative arts ('an art concerned with the design and decoration of objects which themselves may have utilitarian functions and might not be in themselves aesthetically pleasing, for example, ceramics, glassware, textiles, furniture, clothing and architectural details'[3]).

This labelling and the subsequent channelling of academic study has meant that the study of ceramics has been ignored by almost all in the fine arts field. It has become the domain of the archaeologist, and comment and historical narrative has been made by theorists using the terminology of the crafts. So we have *ceramics* synonymous with *pottery*: A fine example is Peter Dormers seminal book, *The New Ceramics, Trends and Traditions* (Thames and Hudson 1994). Here we have an Introduction by Alison Britton ('British

[3] *Guide to Art*, ed. Shearer West, Bloomsbury 1996

Potter and writer on the applied arts'), then chapters: 'The New Role of the *Potter*', '*Pottery* Form', 'The Painted *Pot*' (in this chapter: '*Decorated* versus *Decorative*'), and 'Unfamiliar *Forms*'.

Specifically, an example from the ceramics world: we have Picasso's 'decorative treatment' of 'ceramic vehicles', and references to 'round plates, and a standard large meat dish used as a field for painted, incised or modelled decoration' (Alan Windsor, *Ceramic Review* 81, 1983). Such is the logic of the applied art credo. This is not a definition or terminology that would be entertained for use in describing his painting on board or canvas, and although some of his ceramics were indeed 'decorative', others were more than that. Compare the above description with a passage from the catalogue *Picasso, Painter and Sculptor in Clay* published to coincide with the 1998 Royal Academy exhibition: '... the series of large round plates that he produced in the 1960s is evidence that he continued to probe the artistic possibilities of clay with enthusiasm. Experiments in relief, in gouging the surfaces and in the varied application of colours resulted in the transformation of plates into heads or faces that are unlike any of his other painting or sculptures in clay or, for that matter, his work in any other media of this period. The power of these haunting faces resides in the expressive possibilities of the ceramic medium itself'.

So, whilst modes of discussion which are made with reference to the form or function of ceramic objects may be completely logical and sound, they are also fundamentally restrictive if they are the only way in which ceramics are studied or viewed.

Another example is the way painting on tiles presents problems for writers on ceramics with this agenda. In 1997 it gave birth to the claim that ceramic surfaces are 'forever a form' and the extraordinary statement that 'tiles are just a cop out' (Linda Sandino, *Studio Pottery* 24, 1997).

The fact is that mark making in the clay surface quite possibly predates clay's use as a material for making pots, and from those earliest days of pot (and tile) making, artists have used the clay surface to paint on. It is inconceivable that all paintings and drawings on pots or tiles have been done by the potters and tilers who made them. It is equally inconceivable that all these ceramics have been viewed as functional objects; indeed from the earliest days it is clear that highly painted pieces of ceramics were used as pictures and wall hangings much in the way that frescoes, tapestries and later oil paintings were.

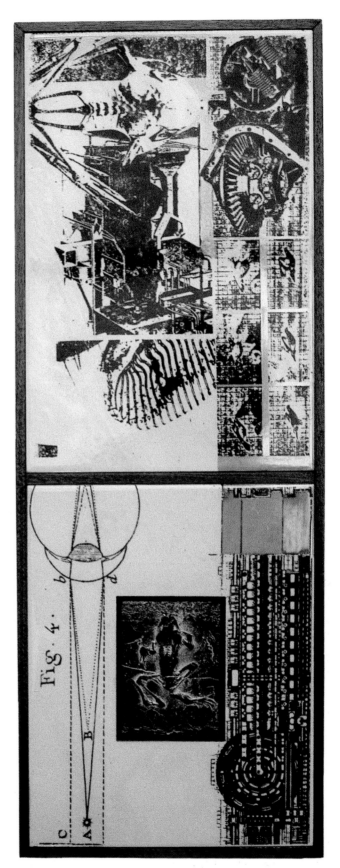

Above Paul Mason (UK), *Comparison Piece 1*, 1996.
'My industrially-produced tiles are like paper bought in the art store.'
(Paul Mason in AN June 1997)

Even the more expansive and open minded Garth Clark in his essay 'American Ceramics since 1950' signifies ceramics as being in two main fields: 'Ceramics has lost its homogeneity. Ceramic sculpture and pottery have become two distinct worlds.' He acknowledges the complexity of the contemporary ceramics scene, but continues: 'The world of the vessel has grown into an artistically credible genre of its own. The sculpture field now has one foot in painting, printmaking, and the sculpture mainstream itself.'

However, as this book will show, there is ceramic work that is neither pottery, nor sculpture. It is painting, drawing or printmaking, but on a ceramic surface, sometimes, significantly, flat. There are many contemporary artists who use ceramic surface not because of its self-referential possibilities, and not because it occupies three-dimensional space or deals with 'volume', but because using slip, underglaze, lustre, onglaze enamel and glazes gives an outstanding palette with which to paint draw and print with.

Not only does the ceramic palette offer extraordinary depths and ranges of colour, but surfaces can have remarkable tactile qualities, and the resulting works have a degree of permanence unobtainable by using any other painting/drawing or printmaking medium. Of course, it is true that there are many contemporary artists who use ceramic materials precisely because of the three-dimensional, and because of the historical references that objects made of clay carry with them. But there is a graphic sensibility, for example, in the work of Cindy Kolodziejski which affects not only the surface but also the form. Here pottery, sculpture and painting collide, and the vocabulary of the applied and decorative arts make a lot more sense, but used alone they still fail to fully describe or comprehend the work.

The element of painting, the materials, techniques, skill and the graphic nature of surface has never been properly discussed, or acknowledged in a way that form or function or clay bodies and glazes have been. This isn't to say that we should plunge headlong into a minute technical analysis of materials and processes, the way in which potters' books do, but there is scope for a look at the varying processes of painting and drawing on clay and glazes, the way they have been used within different genres of work. There is after all a story in which the ceramic surface has evolved graphically. The story is material and technology based early on, but it is also inextricably linked to notions, ideas and works of art. At the end of the 20th century it encompasses a whole body of work that is varied, contradictory, even

Far left and Left Cindy Kolodziejski (USA), *Pajama Party*, 1/98.
Earthenware, slip cast and assembled form, painted underglaze.
36 cm x 18 cm x 10 cm (14" x 7" x 4"). Photo Anthony Cunha,
courtesy Garth Clark Gallery, New York. (Same pot different views.)

*'On this piece I chose the image of a woman giving another woman a
spanking because it was naughty and had kinky soft porn implications.
The open baboon mouth on the other side is savage and to me far more
obscene when you think of the intimacy of looking deep inside a mouth.'*
(Cindy Kolodziejski, September 1998)

*'My moulds come from found objects, my images from found images. T.S. Elliot
once said that lesser artists borrow, great artists steal. Aiming for greatness,
I am a thief, but once I recombine my stolen elements, they are very much my
own . . . Viewers have said that my images are feminist or political, or personal or rooted in the psyche, or ironic or witty or creepy or combinations of some
of these things, but I can't fit them into any one category. I can say though
that whether my images are as cozily domestic as Vermeer's, as lofty as Greek
mythology, or as literal as a biology textbook, an underlying darkness disturbs
their surface serenity. Though I may include a pretty picture, I'm dealing with
bigger issues than prettiness.' (Cindy Kolodziejski quoted in 'Vessel as Canvas'
in* Ceramics Monthly, *September 1995)*

*'I'm going to continue to use cultural materials to present distilled moments
in time. To place the observer in a voyeuristic position, forcing a finish to the
story. The ongoing objective of my work is to create situations which disrupt
perception of everyday reality.' (Cindy Kolodziejski, quoted in 'Pluperfect,
the painted narrative vessels of Cindy Kolodziejski', by Jo Lauria, in*
Ceramics Art and Perception, *No. 19, 1995)*

opposed in intent. It includes fine art, decorative art,
applied art, ceramic art, and ceramic sculpture.

So, this book proposes an alternative version of ceramic history. The first (I think) attempt to plot a painterly
path through history, from Pre-Dynastic Egyptian painting
on pots, through Chinese porcelain, Persian Minai and lus-
treware, Italian maiolica, Delft, the blue and white of the
industrialised West, Soviet propaganda ware, the industrial use of painters and graphic designers, the explorations
of fine artists, and the contemporary scene at the very end
of the 20th century.

With such an overview it is inevitable that omissions
will be made. Historically, there is something of a world
view but, in overviewing the contemporary scene,
Britain, Europe, North America and the Anglo-influenced
tend to dominate. This is mainly because of the difficulties
in accessing information from different cultures and lan-
guages, but also because the contemporary ceramics
'scene' is a product of the Western visual arts economy.
It is a shame though, because 'non-Western cultures tend
not . . . to differentiate between the decorative arts and the

fine arts'[4] and there is surely interesting work out there. It is my wish that any later edition of this book might be more geographically comprehensive in its contemporary and historical overview.

Distilling the history of painting on ceramics into a few chapters has not been an easy task. It is very tempting to set off on detailed accounts of the development of painting styles at particular times and relate how these have affected the art of a period, or influenced the art of another. However I have tried to resist the temptation, for otherwise this book could have taken up volumes. So in the constraints of the space available, I have tried to be as thorough as possible in telling the story, whilst making it accessible, reasonably sound and logical. For those who wish to explore the details of a particular style, time or type of work, there is a bibliography for further detailed investigation.

Before plunging headlong into this narrative, it is necessary to point out that pottery was perhaps the first manufacturing process to be industrialised. There are a considerable number of processes to go through before raw clay becomes a painted pot or tile, and each one of these can be done by different individuals or groups of individuals. There are very early examples of the mass production of drinking vessels: 'drinking cups, some carefully thrown, are all conical or nearly so, rarely more than 6 cm high, and usually undecorated. They are found in very large numbers at Minoan sites from about 2000 to 1360 BC. They have also been found at Mycenaean sites of the 14th century BC'[5].

It is perhaps because of this early potential for mass production, that many painted ceramic pieces throughout history are of low quality materially and artistically. Most were produced without concern for aesthetics, the economic and functional value of the product the main driving force (still true for many industrially-produced wares today). There are however many extraordinarily beautiful, skilfully painted and executed works and it is these, on the whole, that this narrative is concerned with. The makers of these pots and tiles were usually not the ones who painted the surface, and there is clear, written evidence of this at later times. So, the following chapters look at ceramic history from the view of a painter or graphic artist and examine the development of different methods and techniques in the working of ceramic surface, some of the reasons for their use, and the context in which they have been used.

The painters and artists who over the centuries have developed the graphic arts on and in the ceramic surface have all operated within their own time and cultures. Their intentions, their social and economic status varied according to the cultural structure of their age. In viewing the work of the 20th century retrospectively, we see it with different eyes, with all the baggage of history, education and our own preconceptions. However, in selecting the pieces and significant periods in this story, it has been my concern to highlight times when new processes and techniques have led to a noticeable advancement, either in process or content of the work on the ceramic surface. I have also been careful to choose work where the drawn, painted or printed images are more than simply decorative. I have avoided illustrating works where the imagery or patterns on a piece are simply adornments. In short, I have selected works where the painting, drawing or printmaking are quintessential to the pieces' existence: for example, historical pieces where there is a strong element of the narrative, contemporary works where the artists' intentions and ideas are inextricably linked to the graphic development of the ceramic surface.

So, in here you will find little analysis of form or function (unless it specifically relates to the painted/drawn or printed surface). Here you will find the surface, the variety, the marks, lines, shapes, colours . . . and ideas that dominate it.

Finally, and importantly, towards the end of the book, in particular in the chapters that deal with the contemporary scene, I have deliberately used (sometimes extensive) statements or quotes of artists themselves. Too often artists' intentions are filtered through obscure and pretentious writing by others. I have avoided quotations from writers with this tendency, but have included quotes from writers whose comments (I hope) expand and illuminate. As an artist myself I am aware of the problems created when writers and authors misquote or misunderstand one's intentions. I have been very careful to try to be as true as possible to the work and intentions of those whom I have featured and I hope I have succeeded.

There are possibilities here for visual artists from other disciplines. Those interested in the visual arts, and in particular ceramics, painting and printmaking, will find food for thought. I hope this book will tempt many at least to look, and perhaps some, to further explore the possibilities that ceramic materials offer . . . Enjoy . . .

[4] *Guide to Art*, ed. Shearer West, Bloomsbury 1996
[5] Personal correspondence with Vronwy Hankey, June 1995

CHAPTER 1

Naqada, Minai, Greece and Yaozhou, Hui hui ch'ing, Maiolica, and Delft

For much pottery, surface marks, patterns and glazes are simply decorative, adornments to an object which has a simple functional reason for being. But as we look carefully at pieces throughout human history, we see objects that are more than just utilitarian vessels or decorative claddings, there are pieces which tell a story or commemorate an event; objects that are desirable status symbols; political and aesthetic statements, pictures. Indeed, it is partly because of the paintings on some ancient pottery that we know so much detail about the sort of societies that produced them. Writing about Early Greek vase painting, John Boardman explains: ' . . . the evidence of painted pottery is of historic value beyond its intrinsic interest, since we are at the dawn of the historic period in Greece, when texts are scarce and later records unreliable, so that archaeology has to fill out the picture of what was happening in the Greek world'[6].

The earliest manifestations of painting have been found on cave walls of the western Mediterranean (dating back some 35,000 years), and although carvings in walls, modelled figures and heads have been discovered in ages since then, the art of painting itself appears to have been restricted by the lack of a technology to adequately facilitate what we now perceive as a significant human activity. It is possible of course that painting existed on more environmentally fragile materials than clay, but materially, naturally, there is little physical evidence of this.

Below White decorated bowl showing three large horned bovids with young around stylised pool. Ex Howard Carter Collection 1946. 297 Naqada (5" dia.) and Beaker showing two Barbary sheep (with chest mane), three bovids, three smaller animals without horns, two double peaked hills and two unidentified painted objects. E2778 Hu or Abadiya Naqada 1. Ashmolean, Museum Oxford.

---

[6] *Early Greek Vase Painting*, John Boardman, Thames and Hudson 1998

Egypt and Greece, the beginnings

In Egypt, the Naqada 1 culture, dating back to 3850–3650 BC appears to produce the first painterly images on clay. Most of the decorated pottery of this ancient time is painted in contrasting coloured slips (liquid clays), with geometric patterns, but there appears a clear break in this purely decorative inclination with an element of narrative appearing showing figures, animals and elements of the landscape.

The technology used by the ancient Egyptians to create simple monochromatic painting used contrasting slips; eventually it became a universal methodology, and evidence of it exists in China by 3000 BC.

Nearer (to Europe), the great Minoan and then Mycenaean civilisations were to adopt the process (presumably as a result of trading) and further develop this simple monochromatic painting, albeit with a limited palette of slips, to create sophisticated flowing paintings over a wide variety of forms.

Painting and figure drawings informed the pots on which they were painted, so for example, funerary urns or grave markers might show a scene of the corpse laid out before the mourners, together with images of the deceased's adventures in life. They 'invite the viewer to engage in the world they view and enter into the fantasy life of the before and after of the picture'; they 'open a dialogue between art and life'[7].

Over a thousand years, an array of painting styles and techniques were developed and refined. They were derived from the use of differing slips and clay bodies, with an increasing use of sgraffito to delineate and sharpen images. Predating the white of Chinese porcelain by some 800 years, a white slip was used as a ground over red or buff bodies which 'eventually allowed a sense of action in space, and the possibility of even ordinary brush strokes showing up strongly against the light background gave scope for a more varied quality of line, and so more expressive drawing'[8].

[7 & 8] *Archaic and Classical Greek Art*, Robin Osborne, Thames and Hudson 1998

Left Early Proto-attic neck-amphora, by the Mesogia Painter, early 17th century BC. 1935. 19. H. 52.5 cm. Ashmolean Museum Oxford.

There are rows of animals at the base of the neck and on the shoulder: horses in one case and deer in the other. The belly of the vase has a procession of chariots, and the neck rows of elegant organically drawn runners. They appear to be like figures in a cartoon strip, frames in a film.

Below right Anne Cummings (Canada) *Artemis Entering the Forest*, 10 cm x 59 cm x 33 cm (4" x 23" x 13"). Greek subjects and mythology still fascinate contemporary ceramists.

'This piece refers to the Greek goddess Artemis, the mythological goddess of the hunt. This reference to Greek mythology is here because my ethnic background is Greek, and this mythology seems somehow part of my ancestry and it is something to celebrate.'

Above Athenian red figure pottery cup (bowl 10" dia. with 2 handles) Found at Orvieto, Italy. Helmet maker. Attributed to the Antiphon painter (5th Century BC, G267 (V518), ARV2339.22). Ashmolean Museum, Oxford.

Above Paul Scott (UK), detail of *Cretan Collage No . 21*, 1988, 'T' material, porcelain with underglaze painting and screen printed decals, lustre. Photo Andrew Morris. Detail shows drawing of warrior from early protogeometric crater, and other images from Heraklion Museum. One of a series of 'ceramic collages', made following time spent in Crete studying Minoan Faience in 1987.

'The Museum in Iraklion had a profound effect on me. I was told I would enjoy all the pottery, but what I wasn't prepared for was the sheer quantity, quality and exuberance of painting on all forms ceramic, from pots to coffins.'

Right Edward S. Eberle, *Cube in a sphere*, 1998, porcelain, 63 cm x 40 cm x 40 cm (25" x 16" x 16"). Photo Jonathan P. C. Eberle.

Eberle constructs thrown and altered, porcelain vessels. He paints on their surface in the same medium used by ancient Greek and Roman painters on pottery: terra sigillata. Working directly onto the surface he produces a painterly maze of overlapping and adjacent nude figures which move around, and sometimes inside, the form.

'All activity contained in the piece comes from the act, comes from the piece itself. In contrast, Greek ware most often depicts a deliberate motif with little or no deviation. One could say that all of my work is a deviation. The compositions are not narrative. Narrative can be likened to a sentence with a Capital at the beginning, has a middle and a period at the end. The sense is linear and is contained within that linear sequence. My work is more like free-form poetry, stream-of-consciousness writing. Non-sequential. No beginning, no middle, no end.' (Edward Eberle, 1999).

15

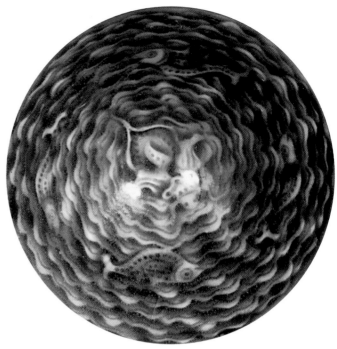

Above Early Yue Ware basin, 3rd or 4th century. Greenish lime glaze, stoneware body. Two fish simply incised, with pecking marks indicating scales. On the outside a diamond diaper band has been impressed with a rouletting tool, and this band is punctuated by four low relief masks which have been sprig moulded and then applied to the surface of the vessel. Dia. 33.1 cm. Percival David Foundation. PDF 250.

Above Small Yaozhou ware bowls with moulded imagery on the inside and incised decoration on the outside. Early 12th century. Dia. 9.7 cm. Interior design of deeply cut waves with four fish swimming around the sides and a monster (possibly a giant squid) emerging from the central area. Outside: incised radiating lines. Percival David Foundation PDF 296 & 297.

Whatever the sophistication and fineness of the Greek ceramics it was at no time glazed, although the slips and engobes used towards the end of the classical period became shiny and almost glaze-like. It was from China that paint and graphics under a glassy, shiny glaze were to appear.

China, Islam and the emergence of glaze and colour

It's not clear whether the development of the white ground used on Greek pottery was known to the Chinese, but the source of the first fine, hard, artificial white ceramic body known as porcelain is China. The significance of the white body and the white ground is that it forms the perfect base for drawn and painted marks. The first examples of cobalt blue and white first appeared in the Gongxian wares of the Tang Dynasty AD 618–906, but examples of these are rare, and the pieces are of poor quality. It was not until the 14th century that underglaze blue of a high standard became established, and this was produced mainly for export [9]. A thousand years before though they were scribing their early high-fired clays with drawn lines, impressed patterns and sprigging in a strong graphic manner: images and line under a glassy layer of glaze.

The extraordinarily fine and translucent porcelain developed in China used together with stable alkaline transparent glazes was to act as a catalyst for a significant change in the Islamic world. It was exported during the Song Dynasty (AD 960–1270), and so valued and sought after was it in the Islamic world that an imitative local ceramic body was created. This was known as *stone paste* or *fritware*. Writing in ad 1301, Abu'l Qasim, historian of the Mongol court and member of a family of potters describes a recipe for this man-made material. 'It is similar in composition to the material commonly referred to as Egyptian paste, and was made from ten parts ground quartz mixed with one part glaze frit and one part fine white clay.' The introduction of the new ceramic body 'was followed within fifty years by a burst of creative energy unparalleled until the rise of Wedgwood and Staffordshire pottery in 18th century England. The extraordinary range of decorative techniques used included wares decorated with mono-

[9] See *Percival David Foundation of Chinese Art, A Guide to the Collection*, Rosemary Scott, p. 66 (Percival David Foundation, London, 1989)
[10] Islamic Tiles, Venetia Porter, British Museum 1995

chrome glazes, wares incised and carved before glazing, wares decorated with moulded and applied ornament and wares painted under and overglaze'[10].

Egyptian paste and similar materials had been used in ancient Egypt, and in Minoan Crete to make figurines, beads, and small graphic tiles. They had a glassy, precious surface in contrast to the everyday pottery which was matt and unglazed. It was a difficult material to form (rather like modelling wet sand I found), and its use disappeared after 330 BC until about the 12th century AD. Rediscovered, Eygyptian paste and its hybrid partner material, stone paste, have since been in almost continuous use in some parts of the Islamic world up to the present day. Later soft paste porcelains, first developed in Florence between 1575 and 1587, are arguably its European descendants.

The early potters developed lead glazes, which in comparison to the alkali, significantly enriched the colours used on the ceramic surface. Unfortunately they also caused painted underglaze colours to melt and run. As a result, the earlier use of coloured slips to apply colour was resurrected. However, the potters of the Abbasid period came up with an alternative solution which involved coating the ceramic surface with an opaque white glaze. Opacifiers included tin and antimony added to lead glazes; alternatively the underfiring of alkaline glazes created a similar effect.

The significance of this white glazed surface was that it provided a relatively stable ground onto which lustres and onglaze colours could be painted. Many metal oxides which make up ceramic pigments are unstable or burn out at temperatures over 1000°C, so colours now referred to as onglaze enamels provide the widest colour palette for the ceramic painter. This is because they are applied to the already vitrified glaze and are low-fired a second time (to about 750°C–850°C), retaining their colour. At this time the technique was known as *minai* (from the Arabic meaning glaze) or *haft rang* (seven, i.e. many colours). Minai pieces were often

Right Bowl, Barlow Gift EA1956.36. Minai ware, stone paste with clear alkaline glaze, and underglaze and overglaze colours, (8"–9"), AD 1180–1220. Ashmolean Museum, Oxford.

bowls, depicting enthroned figures and hunting scenes, some narrative in nature.

Lustres were also used on top of the glaze. Made from oxides of precious metals they produced a shiny metallic sheen on the glazed surface, and were first used on 8th-century glass in Egypt and Syria. They were adapted for use with ceramics in Basra in Iraq in the 9th century. The technique facilitated very fine and graphic painting on the ceramic surface, and its use made a significant contribution to the Islamic arts between the 9th and 14th centuries.

Left Star Shaped Tile: Persia Kashan 13th century AD. Earthenware with opaque white glaze lustre painting. (Burrell Collection, Glasgow Museums and Art Galleries).

visual imagery gradually being replaced by the dominance of arabesque and the calligraphic script.

Whilst in the 'Christian' world there is 'a place for artistic manifestations which are profane and therefore religiously indifferent, but which exist by right (one must give to God that which is God's and to Caesar that which belongs to Caesar) . . . in the world of Islam this separation of life into a religious sphere and a profane one does not exist' (The Arts of Islam, Arts Council 1976). The Koran regulates the fundamental and recurrent facts of everyday life. So as figurative art (so important in European art) is excluded from the liturgical domain it is also excluded from the central core of Islamic civilisation. The pictorial reproduction of nature is not permitted unless it is transformed 'into fabulous imagery so as to make it visibly unreal'. Calligraphic art is of the highest order because it transmits the Koran, the 'divine word' directly revealed in the Arabic language, and it is this that is evident in much Islamic graphic work in ceramics. There are, however, periods of time which do show evidence of narrative painting, particularly in the 17th century in the Safavid period with underglaze painted tiles used in architectural settings.

The Islamic world was also indirectly responsible for the development of blue and white ceramics, so long associated

In the earlier post-Mycenaean Greece, 'we can read, in more detail than in the major arts of sculpture and architecture, the origins of those styles of figure composition and narrative art which, in the full Classical period of the 5th century BC, were to create an idiom destined to determine the future of the arts in the Greek and Roman world, and ultimately in much of the Western world to the present day' (*Early Greek Vase Painting*, John Boardman, Thames and Hudson 1998). In contrast, Islamic art began in this period to take on the characteristics we associate with the arts of Islam today: the depiction of the human figure and narrative

Right Siddig El Nigoumi UK/Sudan, *Guardian Crossword*. Earthenware, burnished bowl with sgraffito drawing.

Siddig El Nigoumi grew up in the Sudan, but lived in England for the last 30 years of his life. On simple forms, he often combined the pictorial with the geometric, describing English subjects and wider issues 'with an iconography that owed much to his African and Arab roots. He embraced a foreign country with a fresh eye that saw the unexpected decorative potential of a motorway junction or crossword puzzle. The formal values in El Nigoumi's work owe much to Islamic art and he had a natural ability to achieve a dynamic asymmetric balance in his decoration.' (Sebastian Blackie in Ceramics Monthly, *1997).*

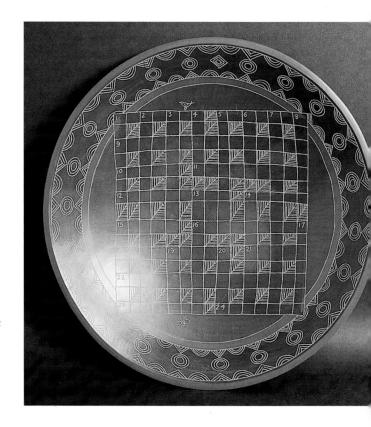

Right Dish with underglaze blue decoration. Xuande mark and period (1426–35). Diameter 17.8 cm (7"). Percival David Foundation PDF B679.

'In the central field on the inside of the dish a writhing dragon has been painted. It is excuted with great vitality in deep blue, the decorator making full use of all the tonal variations at his command. The dragon is shown against a delicately painted background of pale blue waves which provide an effective contrast style of the creature itself. In the cavetto two dragons painted in slip are barely visible. This type of decoration is known as anhua (secret decoration). On the outside of the dish two more blue dragons chase each other among rocks and clouds.' (Percival David Foundation of Chinese Art, A Guide to the Collection.)

with the Chinese. In 1279 Mongol tribes commanded by Genghis Khan's grandson, Kublai Khan, had swept south to conquer China forming the Yuan Dynasty. This consolidated a vast empire stretching from Korea and the Chinese mainland across Central Asia to the Middle East and Europe, westward to the Danube and the Adriatic. Within this huge area, national boundaries disappeared along with all barriers to trade, the exchange of ideas and technologies. So it was that in the 14th century, refined cobalt was exported from the Kashan area of Iran to the Jingdezhen kilns in the Jiangxi province of China where potters began to paint miniature pictures on their unfired clay vessels. Cobalt was referred to as hui hui ch'ing (Mohammedan Blue), and the painted wares were exported to Asia, the Islamic lands and eventually to Europe.

For Islamic countries, the Chinese paintings incoporated Persian compartmentalisation, with the geometric ordering of the ceramic surface, and motifs of flora and fauna from both Chinese and Persian sources. For Europe, the arrangement of imagery was quite different; rather like some multinational corporations of the 1990s, the Chinese

were adept at absorbing and using other foreign influences to their own advantage without fundamentally changing their own aesthetic.

China, and the development of Maiolica and Delft

The blue and white porcelain of this period ('the most revolutionary technical and decorative innovation of the Mongol regime in China, if not in the whole of Chinese ceramic history')[11] was indirectly responsible for the imitative bodies and opaque glazes in the Middle East. In turn, as we shall see later, Europe was affected directly by the Chinese, but it was also indirectly influenced though the spread of the tin glazed, initially to Spain from Arabic North Africa.

Tin-glazed earthenware with lustre (tiles, vases and dishes) was produced in Spain from the 12th century onwards. Many of the painted patterns derived from Islamic sources, coupled with European motifs such as heraldic animals and coats of arms. This ware also made its

[11]'Chinese Ceramics and Islamic Design', *The Westward Influence of the Chinese arts from the 14th to 18th century, Colloquies on Art and Archaeology in Asia*, Percival David Foundation, London, 1973

Above *Noah and the Ark,* 1580, 24.5 cm (9.5") dia. Maiolica painting, Italian (Urbino) or French. Bowes Museum, Barnard Castle, Co. Durham.

Above *Horse and rider,* 1630, 39.5 cm (15.5") dia. Maiolica painting, Italian (Montelupo). Bowes Museum, Barnard Castle, Co. Durham.

way to Italy where there was a strong ceramics tradition originally developed in Roman times, and similar styles were produced. This was known as 'maiolica', the name 'deriving either from Majorca, the island that served as an *entrepôt* for much of the Hispano-moresque ceramics imported into Italy in the 15th century, or from the Spanish term *obra de Málaga* for the imported Malagan Wares [12]'.

It was however, the Italian Renaissance tin-glazed earthenware of the first half of the 16th century that moved the genre on into a completely new area; specifically the painted narrative of *istoriato*. This was 'above all a painter's art, a branch of Renaissance painting as well as a chapter in the history of ceramics: when a piece is said to be 'by' Nicola da Urbino or another, it is the painting which is meant, rather than the throwing of the pot which may have been done by another'[13]. The most famous painters of istoriato were Nicola de Urbino, Orazio Fontana and Francesco Xanto Avelli.

Technically, unlike the earlier Minai ware where painting was on top of the fired glaze, the colours on maiolica were painted on top of the dry (powdery) tin-glazed surface prior to glaze firing. Biscuit fired to about 1000°C, the glaze firing was at a somewhat lower temperature. Sometimes another layer of transparent glaze was applied over the painting, but even if not, the colours sank into the glaze on firing, so that they were much more durable than onglaze enamels. Really this is 'inglaze' painting, and a palette of colours derived from cobalt, copper, manganese, antimony iron and tin gave blues, greens, purple, brown, yellow, orange and white. A further dimension could be added to the painted surface by the additional use of lustres and a third firing.

It is interesting to note that the long held definition of 'fine art' was formed, at the time of these works: 'Painting, sculpture and architecture were not considered by the ancients to be amongst the Liberal Arts, although they were distinguished from mere craftsmanship. A similar confusion existed in the Middle Ages, and the "Intellectualisation" of the arts. Their promotion to "fine" rather than "applied" (decorative arts) – was sanctified by theorists of the Renaissance from Alberti and Leonardo to Vasari and stamped with the approval of the academies' [14].

[12] *Looking at European Ceramics, a guide to technical terms,* David Harris Cohen and Catherine Hess, John Paul Getty Museum/British Museum Press 1993
[13] *Maiolica Italian Renaissance Ceramics in the Ashmolean Museum,* Timothy Wilson, Ashmolean Museum/Christies 1989
[14] *Guide to Art,* ed. Shearer West, Bloomsbury 1996

For the prevailing philosophy of the arts with its increasing technical expertise in the representation of a visually convincing and rationally ordered world, painting on ceramic surfaces, with their pyrotechnically altered colours and brush marks (although obviously not without value) must have seemed so technically inferior to the oils and frescoes of the greats. Had onglaze enamel processes and techniques been as developed then, as they were in 1780 when the 'Eruption of Vesuvius' was painted (see illustration, p.24) it is interesting to speculate whether painting in the ceramic arts might have been higher regarded and placed.

However, significantly, many of the images on ceramics derived originally from paintings and were either straight copies or an artistic interpretation of engravings and undoubtedly some of the painting was very poor. Although there was a growing market for paintings themselves, inevitably this was still concentrated in the hands of the wealthy few; for the less affluent, but growing middle classes, reproductive engraved prints – copies of paintings, reached a far wider market. Their interpretation on ceramic surfaces added a new dimension to the original artworks, and significantly, made the painted image available at a fraction of the cost of the large original paintings. This 'second hand' use of imagery, where 'fine art' pictures are replicated on ceramics became an ongoing feature of European ceramics, and will be examined in further detail later.

Until the late 15th century, most Northern European ceramics were simple, lead-glazed earthenware with minimal imagery and line, any graphic development being created by the trailing use of slips of differing clays. In Northern Italy, to this repertoire was added the incised, sgraffito markings derived originally from China. The process involved coating the thrown or moulded clay object with a white or cream slip through which lines, patterns and textures were incised to reveal the darker body below. 'Piccolpasso noted that this was done with an iron stylus on white clay which came from Vicenza, and described it as sgraffito (scratching). In an alternative technique known as a fondo ribassato, the background was cut away leaving the motifs in white with incised details'[15].

Many of the technical details we know have been gleaned from Cipriano Piccolpasso's book *Three Books of the Potter's Art* published in 1557. He explains in detail the making, glazing and painting processes used in Italian maiolica, makes reference to individual potters and

Top Rimas VisGirda (USA), *The Car we Bought together just began to rust*. Ceramic 1990.

Above Rimas VisGirda (USA), *The Car we Bought together just began to rust*. (Reverse side) Ceramic 1990.

Visgirda's techniques are complex and varied, but, similar in principle to maiolica, he works on a white engobe base. Later drawing and scratching line, shading is achieved with underglaze pencil or liquid underglaze. He also uses lustres and onglaze colours.

'From the Renaissance I saw that it was possible to do narrative on ceramics (maiolica plates), that . . . the two-dimensional reality (especially the development of perspective theory) is an artificial construct.'

[15] *Italian Maiolica and incised slipware in the Fitzwilliam Museum, Cambridge*, Julia E. Poole, Cambridge University Press 1995

describes something of their geographical spread. 'In Flanders, quarried clay is used. I mean at Antwerp, where this art was introduced by one Guido Savino of this place (Castel Durante) and is still carried on at the present by his sons'[16]. It appears that Savino was well established in Antwerp by 1510, and his tiles and other ceramics were well sought after. A floor attributed to him still survives in The Vyne, a Tudor mansion in Hampshire. They are painted in the usual Italian colours of yellow, blue, green and orange, and include paintings of busts of men and women, classical heads amongst the foliage and floral patterns. The significance of Guido Savino is that a number of his sons later moved out of Antwerp to Zeeland in Holland, Seville in Spain and Norwich in England, thus taking the Italian techniques and Italian/Flemish styles with them.

Significantly, this was also the time when the European discovery of printing was leading to an explosion in the availability of the printed word and image. Engravings, mentioned earlier, were widely used in books as illustrations, and it is interesting to note that Antwerp (where Guido Savino had established himself) became a leading topographical centre in the latter half of the 16th century. Trade between Antwerp and Italy became well-established. 'In the 13th and 14th centuries it was principally the Italians who were involved in the paper trade on a large scale which reached our area by way of two large import centres of Bruges and Cologne. From the 15th century it was rather Antwerp which started to oust Bruges from this position, which helps to explain the high concentration of printing businesses in this city'[17].

[16] quoted in *Delftware Tiles*, Hans Van Lemmen, Laurence King 1997
[17] *About Types, Books and Prints*, didactic brochure for the Plantin-Moretus Museum and City Prints Gallery, Antwerp.

Far left Matthias Ostermann, (Canada) *Devil in the Fruit*, platter, brushed and wet blended coloured stain/frit mix with sgraffito drawing through the colour layer into the glaze. 46 cm (18") dia. 1996. Photo Jan Thijs.

Initially trained as a production potter in high-fired stoneware, Ostermann's desire to combine drawing with the clay surface led him to explore the brighter colour palette of low-fire maiolica, which has now become his predominant vehicle of expression. 'It is, to me, a painting medium in its own right, with unique, inherent qualities of colour-blending and light… in my imagery I draw on dreams, human relationships, mythology, stories that I can visualise, and that allow me to create a dialogue with the viewer.'

Above *The Judgment of Paris*, Urbino, from the workshop of Guido Durantino, c. 1545–1550. Acc C.59–1927. Fitzwilliam Museum, Cambridge, T4248.

Left Marcantonio Raimondi's engraving after Raphael's *The Judgment of Paris*. British Museum B, XIV, P197. B/W

23

Above Fragment of dish centre, Venice 1540–1600. Incised line and cutaway areas painted in blue, green, and brown-yellow under lead glaze. Incised slipware dishes decorated with landscapes were the lead-glazed equivalents of the maiolica landscapes mentioned by Piccolpasso as being made in Venice and Genoa. Many fragments of this type were found in the lagoon at Venice Acc No: FMK31787 Fitzwilliam Museum, Cambridge.

So the spread of the printed word, and the printed, engraved image had begun in Europe and from thereon the rate of change on the ceramic surface gathered pace and diversity. The growing availability of printed images impacted on many in society, as Hans Van Lemmen in his book on Delftware tiles observes: 'Painted drawn and printed images have been produced in the Netherlands in abundance from the 16th century onwards. They found their way into many homes as display objects to hang on the wall, or as part of domestic utility ware and material for wall coverings as was the case with Delftware pottery and tiles.' For the increasingly visually literate throughout Europe, there was a demand for ceramics with imagery, and these were not by any means only functional wares with repetitive motif decorations.

Right Harry Juniper (UK): *Jug for the Retiring Bishop of Exeter,* commissioned by the Mothers' Union. 1985. Sgraffito through white slip over red clay body, with transparent glaze (12"/30 cm tall).

Sgraffito reached Northern Europe during the 16th century from Italy. In Bideford in southwest England, potters quickly assimilated the process into their decorative techniques, and distinctive North Devon harvest jugs were produced in periods during the 17th to 19th centuries. Harry Juniper is keeping this North Devon pottery genre alive with contemporary imagery in a traditional form and style.

Above *Eruption of Vesuvius.* Paintings in enamel colours and gilt on soft paste porcelain cup and saucer, c. 1780, Naples (It). Cup 6 cm (2.5") ht, saucer 13 cm (5") dia. Bowes Museum, Barnard Castle, Co. Durham X1853.

Right Portrait, 1779, Schrezhein (Germany). Tin glazed earthenware plaque, high temperature colours, 38.5 cm x 24.5 cm (15" x 9.5").

The Italian subjects of portraiture 'were to have an influence on early 17th century Dutch tiles with busts of Dutch men and women wearing hats, headdresses and the large white collars customary at that time' (Delftware Tiles, Hans Van Lemmen, Laurence King 1997). Although a much later piece, this German tile is a good example of the genre. X1605/1, Bowes Museum. Barnard Castle, Co. Durham.

Delft (named after the Dutch town of Delft) as a definable genre developed around 1600 in Rotterdam (the Netherlands), and in time there were factories making 'Delft' in Britain, Germany, France, Denmark, Portugal and even America. In most cases it seems that the driving force was the imitation of the Chinese blue painting on porcelain. Not having the porcelain body, the tin-glazed earthenware was a cheap substitute, and a hybrid language of imagery and symbols evolved. In addition, unlike the Chinese porcelain which was almost exclusively 'pottery'

(bowls, vases etc.), Delft became synonymous with ceramic tiling, and its popularity spread throughout Europe.

Much Delft was mass produced by factories, with artisan painters copying designs based on engravings, but there were also highly regarded Delft painters, some of whom were commissioned to produce large tiled wall paintings in blue and white. Examples of large-scale tile paintings can be found from Persian and Islamic architectural tiling on the outside and inside of buildings, (mainly geometric or calligraphic in content) through to Spain, Italy and Portugal, thence on to Northern Europe.

In Portugal azulejos (glazed polychrome tiles) are an important element of the country's visual art culture and history: 'Used continuously throughout Portugal's history

Below *De Leydsche Dam Plaque,* c.1753. Delft (Holland), tin-glazed earthenware, high temperature colours, 22 cm (8.5") ht. Depicting and commemorating the building of the Leydsche Dam in 1753. X4363, Bowes Museum, Barnard Castle, Co. Durham.

Above Birds in cages, Delft, tin-glazed earthenware plaques, high temperature colours, c. 1750, 25.5 cm (10"), and 14.5 cm (5.5").

The depiction of birds on Dutch tiles was a widespread phenomenon and in the 18th and 19th centuries tile panels with canaries and parrots in cages appeared. X4327-8, Bowes Museum, Barnard Castle, Co. Durham.

Above Plate, *Christ and the Adulteress*, after Martin de Vos, Dutch (perhaps Haarlem) c. 1630, tin-glazed earthenware. 39.5 cm (15.5") dia.

The depiction of biblical scenes was a popular subject for paintings on ceramics since the Italian Renaissance. In rural Protestant Holland and northern Germany they were particularly popular. X1545 Bowes Museum, Barnard Castle, Co. Durham.

over a period stretching back to the Middle Ages, the azulejo has acquired renewed vigour, while reflecting the organic eclecticism of a culture that was both expansive and open to dialogue. It has embraced the lessons of Moorish artisans and was inspired by the ceramics of Seville and Valencia. It later adapted the ornamental formulae of the Italian Renaissance, while not ignoring the exoticism of oriental china, and, following an ephemeral period of Dutch inspiration, it created fantastic story-panels in blue and white that set the tone for a perfect assimilation of such varied elements' [18].

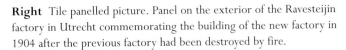

Right Tile panelled picture. Panel on the exterior of the Ravesteijin factory in Utrecht commemorating the building of the new factory in 1904 after the previous factory had been destroyed by fire.

The painting probably represents the Roman goddess Minerva, protector of the arts and crafts, holding a small statue of Venus de Milo and an artist's palette symbolising sculpture and painting. At her feet are ceramic products such as vases and tiles while a pottery kiln can be seen in the background. Photo courtesy Hans Van Lemmen. Painting on tiles is one of the aspects of ceramic history (and current practice) that those proponents who argue that all ceramics must be considered as 'objects' or 'vessels' conveniently forget, or dismiss.

[18] Portuguese Tiles from the National Museum of Azulejo, Lisbon, João Castel-Branco Pereira, Zwemmer/Instuituo Portgués De Museus, 1995

CHAPTER 2

Enamels, Paste, Porcelain, China and Willows

As we have seen, much of the graphic innovation of the ceramic surface came about because of the ceramics coming out of China. There, situated on a vast plain where large lakes connected by canals make easy access to the Yangtze River, the 'porcelain capital' was the town of Jingdezhen. 'By the 18th century it was an industrial stronghold of worldwide importance with a population of over a million people, only Venice was larger'[19]. Fuel for kilns was readily available and to the east of the town the Matsang Mountains provided a plentiful source of Kaolin (white china clay) and Baidunzi or Petunsteth (white feldspathic mineral) the raw materials needed to make porcelain. These were discovered in China around 1700 BC, nearly three and a half thousand years before they became available in Europe (around AD 1710).

Left Group of three dishes, Chinese Qing Dynasty Kangxi period AD 1700. Porcelain, underglaze cobalt blue painting, 8" (20 cm) dia. each. Made at Jingdezhen kilns in Jiangxi province. From a larger set. The central images are taken from a drama called *The West Chamber* (Xixiangj). Burrell Collection, Glasgow Museum and Art Galleries.

It tells of the love between scholar Zhang and Gui Yingying who meet at the monastery of Universal Salvation while Yingying, her mother and maid are staying there. The love is encouraged by Yingying's scheming maid, but opposed by her mother who thinks that a poor scholar is not good enough to marry her daughter. Scholar Zhang leaves to go to the capital to sit the state exams and after various adventures he returns to claim his bride.

[19] *Blue and White China, Origins / Western Influences*, Rosalind Fischell, Little Brown and Co 1987

Above and right Charles Krafft (USA), three plates from the series, *Darkness in Delft* 1993. Painted onglaze on production stoneware, 30.5 cm x 23 cm (12" x 9") approx. Using plates as canvas, or picture strip, Krafft has created the sense of a narrative in these plates. Unlike the Chinese narrative this one has more sinister overtones.

Direct trade with China was non-existent in the early Middle Ages, but the Italian explorer, Marco Polo (1254–1324) wrote a detailed account of a land called Cathay after a mammoth nine year trading trip to Asia. At first ridiculed, it eventually became the subject of much fascination, as the products of this distant land gradually began to appear. In the 14th century, Chinese porcelain in Europe was still extremely rare, and these dazzling, glazed, pure white, fine translucent objects with paintings of birds, animals, insects, and plants in intense blue were simply the most exotic and wonderful objects. Together with stories emerging of far off riches and strange peoples, and compared with the chunky, heavy, simple, lead-glazed earthenware used in Northern Europe, the porcelains must have seemed to have come from a completely different world. Today, when industry has made it available and familiar to all, it is hard to understand the value placed on them, rather like trying to comprehend the hysteria that gripped

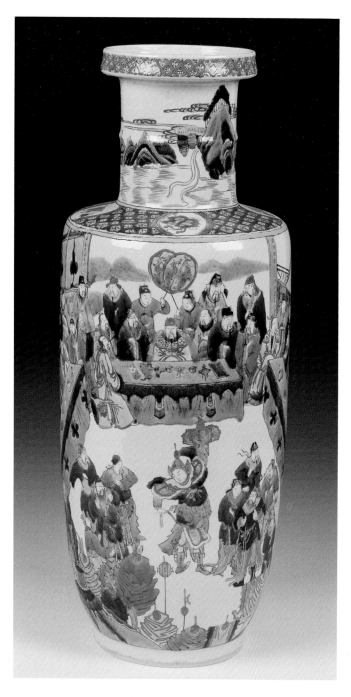

Above Story Vase. Chinese Qing Dynasty Kangxi period, AD 1700. Porcelain, 60 cm (24") tall, onglaze famille verte enamels. Made at Jingdezhen kilns in Jiangxi province. 38/886 Burrell Collection, Glasgow Museums and Art Galleries.

The vase depicts the final scene of the Water Margin (Shuiluizhaun). The story is set in the early 12th century, and tells of hero Song Jiang who leads a group of 108 bandits against the actions of a corrupt government. Their loyalty to the emperor (although, not his ministers) eventually results in their pardon and their fighting for the emperor against other rebels and invaders. The final scene in the story shows the imperial banquet held in their honour following their successful defeat of the Khitan Tartars when all but 27 of the group were killed. Around the neck of the vase is depicted the original marshland hideaway of Song Jiang in Shaudong province.

the Dutch in the 'tulipomania' of the 17th century, when a single tulip bulb changed hands at a price equivalent to 60 times the average income, or the cost of a house in the best area of Amsterdam (*The Tulip*, Anna Pavord, Bloomsbury 1998).

European explorers later opened up trade routes to the East by sea. However, the immediate effect of Chinese porcelain ware on European ceramics (as we have seen) was to encourage the production of a range of imitative products and surface treatments which ultimately produced genres of work with their own aesthetic and traditions (maiolica, Delft).

Porcelain and Europe

Eventually, between 1575 and 1800, a variety of porcelain, or porcelain-like bodies were discovered or invented in Italy, France, Germany and England. Soft Paste Porcelain, a substitute body akin to the earlier 'Fritware' or 'Stone Paste' produced in Iran was developed and used in the Medici factory in Florence from around 1575. Later versions were used in France and other parts of Italy. (This body was made by mixing ground glass and white clays, firing to around 1200°C to vitrify them, then crushing and grinding the resulting mix which was then in turn combined with plastic clays to make it malleable. Transparent lead glazes were used, and the surface provided the perfect base for onglaze enamel painting. However, losses in the kiln were high; an accurate measurement of kiln temperature was not possible until the invention of pyrometric cones in the 19th century by a German, Hermann August Seger). Hard paste porcelain first appeared in 1709 in Meissen, Germany, and later at the end of that century, in England, Josiah Spode marketed a version since known as bone china (ash of calcined ox bones were added to the paste making a very white and translucent porcelain body. High biscuit fired to 1280°C, the glaze firing is at a lower temperature of 1080°C–1100°C. This process ensures that the high firing, potentially causing the most damage, is done before the application of any painted underglaze or onglaze).

Detailing the technical aspects of these innovations might seem an irrelevance to a book devoted to the surface and graphics, perhaps falling into the peculiarly ceramic habit of obsessing with materials, process, recipes and techniques. However, the significance of the development of these porcelain bodies is that they allowed not only the production of 'finer' forms, but also provided the pure white base on which different techniques of painting, drawing and later printing would be significantly developed. It is the consistent whiteness and smooth nature of the ground

which allowed and encouraged the development of painterly and graphic techniques. In the fine art world, early fresco painters, and then later the Pre-Raphaelites and Impressionists, understood that a white ground gives an unmuddied base on top of which pigments can be painted and mixed to best effect, giving pure, bright colours. Their use of colour was revolutionary at the time. It is interesting to speculate whether the pure bright colours of painted porcelain in any way influenced their decisions to use a white ground.

Onglaze painting, first developed on Minai ware in the 11th century, reappeared on Chinese porcelains in the late 17th and early 18th centuries. Two categories of enamelled wares are known as *famille verte* and *famille rose*[20]. Famille verte was a range of mainly transparent colours, aubergine, blue, yellow and green (from which the vert comes), with two opaques, black and iron red. The famille rose palette included a rose pink enamel (made using colloidal gold) and two opaque colours, yellow and white. These were particularly important because they allowed for the blending of

[20] Coined by Jacquemart and Le Blant in their book *The History of Porcelain* published in Paris in 1862. Described in *Percival David Foundation of Chinese Art, A Guide to the Collection,* Rosemary Scott. Percival David Foundation of Chinese Art, School of Oriental and African Studies, University of London, 1989.

Top Painting, on hard paste porcelain plate, c. 1730. Jingdezhen (China), dark enamel and gold. In 18th century Europe, there were few porcelain factories, and many wealthy Europeans used to commission dinner services direct from China, sending engravings for use as subject matters. This plate with an obviously non-Chinese subject matter is one such piece. X4515, Bowes Museum, Barnard Castle, Co. Durham.

Centre Dessert Plate, c. 1810. Paris (France). Hard paste porcelain with coloured enamels and gold. Unmarked. X2408 Bowes Museum, Co. Durham.

Left *Hope Service:* detail of oval serving dish, *Flight,* Worcester 1792 (for the Duke of Clarence). Onglaze, monochromatic painting, painted by John Pennington with a female representing Hope and Patience. Courtesy of the Trustees of the Museum of Worcester Porcelain.

31

other colours thus creating a pastel palette. In making their appearance in Europe together with Japanese Imari and Polychrome porcelains, it was not long before the technology of onglaze enamels was used on the new European porcelains and tin-glazed wares. By 1749 the Vicennes factory in France (later to become Sèvres) boasted a palette of 60 colours.

Porcelain was produced by a relatively small number of factories, several under Royal Patronage. Meissen (Germany) and Sèvres (France) are two of the most famous. Over the next 150 years skilful artists, working for factories (usually anonymously), used increasingly sophisticated techniques and palettes, and produced some astounding painted images on porcelain surfaces. Many large paintings on tiles were undertaken and framed as if oil paintings.

Although many were original compositions, many were also copies of, or 'after' well-known paintings. The Sèvres Museum contains more than 40 porcelain plaques made between 1817 and 1840, and so determined were they that the works should be faithful to the originals that artists were sent to Rome in order to copy the frescoes of Raphael and his school in the Vatican. One of the largest

Above *George Stubbs ...*
Josiah Wedgwood, 1780. Enamel painting on Wedgwood biscuit earthenware plaque, 50.1 cm x 41 cm (20" x 16"). Inscribed 'Geo. Stubbs Pinxit 1780'. Courtesy Trustees of the Wedgwood Museum, Barlaston, Staffordshire, England.

Right Landscape, unknown painter, 1880–1885. 51 cm x 57 cm (20" x 22 ½"), onglaze enamel on ceramic tile. Zsolnay, Janus Pannonius Múzeum, Pécs, Hungary.

panels is a painting by Moïse Jaccober: Pyramid-shaped bouquet and basket of fruit after the original by Van Spaendonck commissioned by Louis XVI. The original painting was later housed in the French Embassy in Berlin and was a casualty of the Second World War, but the copy on porcelain survives at Sèvres. This hints at one advantage the ceramic has over oil or watercolour pigments and associated materials. Providing it is not dropped and broken, the ceramic will survive in exactly the same state as it was when it came out of the kiln (Chinese porcelain in perfect condition is still being exhumed from the depths of the South China Sea from the wrecks of boats of the Dutch and East India companies from the 1700s.). Colours on the ceramic surface, being mineral based, fused in glaze or frit, are much less susceptible to atmospheric pollution, the effects of ultraviolet light or damage by fire, than conventional painting where vegetable or other pigments in binders and mediums change colour over time, and backing or ground materials deteriorate, requiring restoration, which at best is expensive, and at worst is expensive and controversial. True, the ceramic can be fragile, and comparatively heavy, but the sustainability of colour is an appealing asset.

Above Børsen painting on hard paste porcelain, in enamel colours and gilt. Diameter 20 cm (8"). Denmark (Copenhagen), c. 1867, X3031.2. The Bowes Museum, Barnard Castle, Co. Durham.

Left Porcelain table originally in the collection of King Louis Philippe of France, painted by Jean Charles Develly. Illustrated with scenes from Milton's *Paradise Lost*. Table designed by Jean Charles Francois Leloy. The Gothic revival style used for this piece was highly fashionable in the 1820s. L1/87 Bowes Museum, Co. Durham.

Left One of a pair of vases, French, 1853, Sèvres porcelain, blue celeste with panels painted by Jean Charles Develly. Bowes Museum, Co. Durham.

Right Richard Milette, one of a pair of lidded baluster vases, earthenware, 43 cm x 30 cm (17" x 12"). Collection of Candice Groot, Illinois USA. Photo Raymonde Bergeron.

Milette's use of ground colour is based on those used at Sèvres during the reign of Louis XV. All the shards are fabricated rather than actual, and are designed to invoke memories of the varied surfaces employed in world ceramics. 'Richard Milette probes the indoctrination endemic in the field of study, that for a ceramist, hard paste porcelain must always mean exquisite and the exceptional, and that Sèvres pictorial mythological boudoir melodramas must always feature heterosexual seductions. The rigidity of Sèvres shapes is used by the artist as metaphor for the severity of attitude in the experiences of formal education, of socially or "politically correct" attitude, and of inflexible social structures. Milette lays bare the antithetical in today's mores and the complexities involved in actual social change.

While his pieces are on one level indeed about material and the status of material, the artist actually used a low-fired white clay body, rendering them trompe l'oeil ceramics in a conceptual sense, and even the painted surfaces and the artist's use of colour are not imitative, rather they are borrowed.' Gloria Lessing, 'Ceramics, Richard Milette', Contact Magazine No. 87, 1991.

Above *Landscape* by Kinkozan Sobei VII, c. 1885. Earthenware plate, 36.7 cm (14.5"), painted with landscape in westernised perspective, in polychrome enamels and within a lobed border. Signed Kinkozan; Kyoto, Japan. Photo courtesy Ashmolean Museum, Oxford (1992.71 Story Fund).

Right Robert Dawson (UK), *In Perspective,* 1996. Inglaze screen print on bone china plate 25 cm (10") dia. A trompe l'oeil, a three-dimensional illusion created on a self referential three-dimensional object.

The extraordinary achievements of the finest porcelain factories and artists in creating a palette and process to rival the luminosity and graphic detail of oil painters was exclusively for the aristocracy and the very wealthy. The depiction of pastoral and classical scenes, together with chinoiserie served as 'fanciful embellishment in the Age of Reason, a supposedly scientific age'[21].

The introduction of print

At the same time as the aristocracy were receiving their commissioned dinner services, vases and porcelain paintings, factories were producing increasing amounts of ceramic wares for other markets. The invention of other substitute white or cream earthenware bodies, and the mechanical and industrial revolution, facilitated the mass production of good quality wares at cheaper and cheaper prices. The adaption of printing processes for use in ceramic decoration made the next big impact on the graphic nature of the ceramic surface. Here the driving force was primarily economic: printing meant that the mass produced could also be decorative, and decorative meant desirability and sales.

Earliest prints were produced from wood blocks, but soon most were made from copper engravings which produced finer lines and more subtle qualities. At first they were transferred with a glue or gelatine pad, and then with a fine pottery tissue, a process which enabled a greater density of ink to be applied; it was more robust and

[21] 'Ceramics, Richard Milette', Gloria Lessing, *Contact Magazine*, No. 87, 1991

Above Robert Dawson (UK), from: *Can you walk from the garden, does your heart understand?* 1996. Inglaze screen print on bone china plate 10" (25 cm) dia.

'Dawson has appropriated a universally familiar ceramic image, deconstructed it in various ways and re-presented its component subject matter – the pagoda, the birds in flight the figures crossing the bridge – in new graphic arrangements that are immediately arresting …
A comparison with pop music is not inappropriate. The principle of

sampling (or stealing) tiny but recognisable sections of previous recordings for new compositions has become a standard production method in contemporary pop. The use of photography, the photocopier and/or the computer not to invent, but to reproduce, distort and rearrange digital information, whether visual or aural is not confined to any one discipline. With the willow pattern plates, Dawson is signalling that he can use computers as intelligently as other potters might use a sable brush, or a musician might use a musical instrument', Paul Vincent, Studio Pottery 25/26.

precise, and soon became the standard method of applying graphic imagery.

The quality of a printed reproduction depends on a number of factors. It is not only the quality of the original copperplate engraving from which the print is made, but also the materials and process used to achieve the successful print; the pigment, the transfer of sufficient colour from plate via transfer material to the ceramic surface, the glaze through which an underglaze or inglaze print shows and the firing, all affect the final result. Printmaking is, as anyone who has tried it will tell, an exact art, and there is a very fine line between success and failure. With all the additional hurdles for the ceramic printer, it must have taken many, many tests with materials and machines to get prints to work at all, let alone consistently.

In the case of underglaze blue, the main pigmentation was cobalt. Glaze has an effect on the brilliance of the blue colour, but unfortunately the more brilliant the glaze, the more solvent the glaze action; so it is unusual to find underglaze blue without a degree of blurring. (In some cases this was encouraged by the addition of salt, lead and calcium carbonate in the firing, producing 'flow blue', in which a diffused blue haze surrounds the printed image. Flow blue was fashionable during periods of the 19th century.) Over time technical problems were resolved, and the technology and skills developed to a very fine level. (A detailed account

Right Michael Keighery (Australia), *Willow Pattern Shard*, 14" x 18" (35 cm x 40 cm). Inlaid earthenware with assembled fragments.

'These shard/plates invite viewers to engage on a number of levels; to become cultural travellers and at the same time to recognise their own position in relation to the significance of familiar objects; to look beyond the surface of the familiar to the historical and aesthetic foundation which supports cultural recognition', 'Michael Keighery's Shards of Memory', *Marilyn Walters* Ceramics Art and Perception, *No. 33, 1998.*

Below Leopold Foulem (Canada), *Cylindrical Blue and White Teapot in Silvered Mounts,* 22.7 cm x 23.5 cm x 17.5 cm (9" x 9.25" x 7") Ceramic and found objects. 1995/96. Photo Raymond Bergeron.

of the development of printing materials and methods can be found in Robert Copeland's *Spode's Willow Pattern and other designs after the Chinese*, Cassell 1990.)

Images on these early pieces were taken from popular engravings (still used as the primary source of image reproduction, and illustration in books), and adaptations and versions of the Chinese images imported on porcelain (*chinoiserie*). As we have seen, the Chinese used forms, bowls and plates for narrative and compositional pictures, as well as providing vehicles for simple or complex decorative designs. These designs, associated in the minds of Europeans with blue and white pottery, were naturally desirable images to use on the new mass produced wares.

In England, proliferating pottery factories produced a whole series of designs based on Chinese iconography. In these, the narrative and the decorative merged. Perhaps the most famous and lasting design produced is the now world famous, Willow Pattern. The border details were derived from traditional Chinese designs (standardised on Canton and Nanking export porcelains), but were concocted in Stoke-on-Trent in England. There is some dispute as to the original designers, but it seems that Spode was the first factory to transfer print the image in 1785. The legend itself contains a bridge (with three or five arches), three people crossing it, a willow tree, an orange tree, a boat, a tea house, two birds and a fence across the foreground of the garden. It is a story of two eloping lovers pursued by the girl's father. In Buddhist iconography the willow tree symbolises meekness, it is a symbol of spring and also represents woman. The orange tree (which should bloom all year round) is regarded as a bringer of good luck. Both plants are given as gifts at the Lunar Year [22].

Produced in millions over the years, it is bizarre that this image (in differing versions) has become the most reproduced in ceramic history, the meaning, symbolism and story lost and irrelevant to most. 'The pattern as a cultural sign is the culmination of three centuries of European fascination with, and large scale appropriation of, the Oriental. It also represents a popular idea of traditional Chinese culture, made accessible to millions of English and European diners through mass produced tableware. The story of the Willow Pattern is the universal story of forbidden love, made exotic for European consumption' [23].

Alongside the imitative and decorative, a strong tradition of commemoration and political commentary developed. In Britain, 'the transfer print enabled the pottery factories to respond quickly to the issues of the day and certain characters became the subject of large quantities of pottery. In the early 19th century national heroes such as Lord Nelson and later the Duke of Wellington were popular, while the trials and tribulations of the Royal Family were also a rich source of ceramic imagery . . . Ceramics were used to sway public opinion and promote political causes such as the Catholic Emancipation campaign, the Anti-Slavery campaign. The great Reform Bill of 1832 was the most prolifically recorded political event in ceramic wares . . . Printed ceramics were a product of the new urban societies of the 19th century, catering for tastes for the topical and the titillating but also a vehicle for the dissemination of ideas around public issues and party politics' [24].

The overt politicisation of the ceramic surface through image and text was to be an integral part of the next, literally revolutionary, change in the marriage of art and porcelain.

[22] *Spode's Willow Pattern and other designs after the Chinese*, Robert Copeland, Cassell 1990
[23] Marilyn Walters, 'Michael Keighery's Shards of Memory', *Ceramics Art and Perception*, No. 33, 1998
[24] Moira Vincentelli in *Hot Off the Press*, ed. Paul Scott, Bellew 1996

Above Steve Bell and Stephen Dixon, *Annus Horribilis*.
Glazed Earthenware with decal.

CHAPTER 3

Bolsheviks and Baltars, Wedgwood and Wilson. Artists, Production and the Ceramics Industry

In the area of the fine arts devoted to painting, there is an accepted history of significant artists and movements. Similarly, in the 20th century a catalogue and shared body of knowledge about the fine arts exists. However the same cannot be said of ceramics with a graphic content, where differing dominant philosophies have meant the exclusion of a whole areas of practice from the accepted historical narrative.

The early exclusion of all ceramic practices and traditions from the definition of the fine arts did without doubt contribute to a downgrading of the value of paintings and graphics associated with the medium. There are few famous ceramic painters, and until recently no clearly identified significant movements or times. The study of (ceramic) painting practice and methodology was not taught in the academies, and most graphically gifted individuals were, as a result, steered to careers in the fine arts (still true today). In addition, the opportunity to develop skills and careers in ceramic painting and printmaking was until the 20th century, severely restricted by access to the necessary materials, knowledge and technology. Painters simply needed studio space, canvas, board and paints. For ceramics, the materials and technology were more com-

plex, and until the late 20th century were only available in factories or commercial workshops.

So ceramic painting, printmaking and graphics have developed alongside and inside industrial production. Wealthy patronage was not willing or prepared to pay for adventurous experimentation, nor were there outlets for such innovation and expression had they even existed. The revolutionary movements in painting, the Pre-Raphaelites, Impressionism, Post Impressionism, Cubism etc. had an arena in which innovation, although not at the time accepted, had an opportunity to be exhibited and noticed. There was a visual art economy, with galleries, salons, spaces and institutions that fed it. Gradually this market became aware of the saleability of innovation, the new, and the shocking. The exclusion of ceramics and other so-called applied arts meant that innovation in these areas was slower, and tended to reflect the fashions, tastes and movements outside the genre. This helps to explain the rather imitative nature of much ceramic painting. Painting and the graphic arts in ceramics were held back, both by material and technological circumstance, and the associations and markets that have provided the audience, customers and latterly, the critics.

Soviet Propaganda Ware

The Bolshevik Revolution of October 1917 was to change all that. The Mongols centuries before had swept into China destroying culture and tradition, but they had (perversely) also acted as catalysts for great innovation and change in Chinese, and world, ceramics. Similarly, the Russian Revolution which also destroyed many traditions and lives, also produced the most revolutionary art, and porcelain, in more than one sense.

For the Bolshevik government, whose control of Russia was extremely precarious in the period immediately following the Revolution, propaganda was of critical importance in maintaining and developing a hold on power. The potential power of the visual arts were valued early on. The head of the Narkompros (the 'People's Commissariat for Public Enlightenment', responsible for the administration of Education and the Arts) was made a member of the Bolshevik inner circle with direct access to Lenin. Artistic proposals and practice were promoted, defended and justified at the highest level in the new government. Artists were urged to leave their easels and help in the drive to educate and inform the populace, and to promote the goals of the Revolution.

This was in an age before radio and mass communication, and so to disseminate information and galvanise political and economic activity, *agitprop* (from the Russian *agitatsaya propaganda* (agitation propaganda), used by Lenin in a 1902 pamphlet, suggesting methods of agitation and propaganda for the achievement of political ends) trains, ships and trucks were systematically dispersed around the country. Painted with revolutionary images and slogans, each train was equipped with a printing press for the production of revolutionary pamphlets, a book-shop and small library for the literate, a gramophone for broadcasting Lenin's speeches and a coach fitted out for meetings, the showing of propaganda films and performed propaganda plays.

Newspapers were scarce in the war-ravaged country but their absence was overcome with the creation of political posters and wall newspapers which were displayed in store windows. In 1919 the artist Mikhail Cheremnykh devised a version of the wall newspaper which incorporated the latest news in telegraphic style, juxtaposed with printed cartoons – satirical sketches that were subsequently hand painted or stencilled. Other artists joined Cheremnykh in producing the ROSTA (Russian Telegraph Agency) windows which were changed at least weekly and sometimes more frequently.

It is against this background that the former Imperial Porcelain Factory was employed to produce, the now famous, Propaganda Porcelain. Established in the early part of the 18th century, at a similar time to the other great European porcelain factories, it had produced work exclusively for the imperial court for over 150 years. It was renamed the State Porcelain Factory in 1917 (it became the Lomonosov Porcelain Factory in 1925 and is still in production today) but no clear mandate for its production was clear in the early post-revolutionary days. Nina Lobanov-Rostovsky explains: 'The Bolsheviks had given relatively little thought to the way in which they would administer the country after taking over. Immediately after the October Revolution many pragmatic decisions had to be taken in education, art and industry. There was no overall set pattern of administration. In many cases specialists were able to keep the jobs they had held before the Revolution. This was the case at the Imperial Porcelain Factory, where the reorganisation took place fairly swiftly and smoothly. After the February Revolution it had come under the aegis of the Ministry of Trade and Industry of the new regime which took absolutely no notice of it. Everyone at the factory stayed on, and in theory it was ruled by a workers' control commission. Artists and sculptors ranked as workers, so there was no "class" problem' [25].

Sergei Vasilievich Chekhonin, elected to the post of artistic director, set about recruiting additional artists, some famous, some unknown, to work for the art department of the factory. Rudolf Feodorovich Vilde was already head of painting. He was joined amongst others by Mikhail Adamovich, Alexandra Shchekotikhina Pototskaya and Zinaida Kobyletskaya. In addition, established artists including Natan Altman, Vasilii Kandinsky, and later Malevich and Suetin were to create designs and artworks for porcelain.

Located on the southern outskirts of Petrograd (the city of St Petersburg has undergone a series of name changes. Until the outbreak of the First World War it was known by a semi-German name: St Petersburg. In 1914 the name was Russified to Petrograd, which was in use for ten years until Lenin's death in 1924, when the city was renamed Leningrad. Today it has reverted to St Petersburg), the factory could not be reached by public transport. As there were no living quarters for artists nearby, the artists studio was relocated to the centre of Petrograd in the former Baron A. Stieglitz Central School of Technical Design.

[25] *Revolutionary Ceramics, Soviet Propaganda Ware* 1917–1927, Nina Lobanov-Rostovsky, Laurence King 1990

'The artists worked at two long tables in a room that was often freezing – there was not always fuel for the Franklin stove, which, even when burning could not heat the vast room properly. Frequently the artists had to work with their coats and mittens on. However, they later remembered it as an exciting and exhilarating time, despite the hardships and the food and fuel shortages and they managed to express some of this excitement in their work. They were aware that they were part of an important propaganda campaign and that their art had a valued place in Soviet life' [26].

One of the early difficulties faced by the Bolsheviks was a basic shortage of materials for the propaganda campaign. In the porcelain factory this was not an immediate problem because there was a huge stock of unpainted plates ready to be covered in revolutionary slogans and themes. The factory had produced dinner services, platters, jugs, teapots, cups and saucers in anticipation of future orders, stockpiling them so that when the imperial word was received the painting could begin on a ready-made canvas. In stores they found assorted stamped wares going back to Nicholas I (1825–1855).

A new State Porcelain Factory stamp of a hammer, sickle and cog was designed by Alexis Eremeevich Karev. At first the existing imperial back stamps were covered with an oval or diamond shaped patch of green or black enamel, before stamping with the new logo, but later, the state factory stamp was simply used alongside the imperial.

Above Sergei Vasilievich Chekhonin: large dish known as *Famine*, 1921. Photo Courtesy of Sothebys.

Making clear references to the Russian ikon tradition, this piece portrays a pale green grieving mother/Madonna in a black and gold veil, with two starving children. Chekhonin regarded it as one of his masterpieces. Chekhonin, trained as a painter and a ceramicist, made a number of maiolica panels in Moscow and Petrograd. He worked on illustrations for magazines and books, and was considered the most outstanding book illustrator in pre-revolutionary Russia. He was active in the World of Art Group in Petrograd. His graphic work on ceramics was astonishingly varied, having a respect and attachment to the past, but an enthusiasm for contemporary innovative trends in art. From 1918 to 1923, and 1925 to 1927 he was the director of the State Porcelain factory in Petrograd. Responsible for the recruitment of many of the factory artists, he was an inspirational motivator of others. He also designed postage stamps, paper and silver money, jewellery and posters. He emigrated to Paris in 1928, and worked as designer for cabaret and ballet; he also worked for Vogue magazine. Chekhonin's work 'was the backbone of revolutionary porcelain.

Many artists, designers and decorators followed his lead, producing a style that fundamentally changed the nature of porcelain decoration in a remarkably short space of time. Chekhonin's influence lasted barely ten years, yet during that time he was able to make porcelain the most avant-garde of all the forms of decorative art, giving to tablewares … a relevance that they had never enjoyed before' (Paul Atterbury 'A Revolutionary Collection' Ceramics, the International Journal of Ceramics and Glass, Feb/March 1986).

The basic new stamp, the symbols of which were sometimes differently placed in relation to each other.

[26] *Revolutionary Ceramics, Soviet Propaganda Ware 1917–1927*, Nina Lobanov-Rostovsky, Laurence King 1990

Left Alexandra V Shchekotikhina Pototskaya, *Motherhood Plate.*

Shchekotikhina came from a family of 'Old Believers', whose traditional crafts were ikon painting, book illumination, and embroidery. She studied at art school in Petrograd, where she was funded to tour northern Russia studying indigenous art forms. Her love and knowledge of visual Russian folk traditions encouraged her to 'disregard perspective, and her plates and cups and saucers are painted with all events occurring emphatically on the surface. There is no distance in Shchekotikhina's work. Contrast with gold leaf stresses the distinct quality of the joyous enamelled colours employed, and despite the lack of pictoral structure, her designs are full of energy and impetuous rhythm with exaggerated figures and objects' (Revolutionary Ceramics, Soviet Propaganda Ware 1917–1927, Nina Lobanov-Rostovsky, Laurence King 1990). She travelled widely, lived in Paris for a time, and she also worked on designs for costumes and decorations for opera.

Right Z. W. Kobyletskaya, *Newspapers,* Petrograd 1921. Painted onglaze enamel on porcelain. Inv No 74/50. Photo courtesy Badisches Landesmuseum Karlsruhe, Germany.

Referencing the use of newspapers for disseminating information. Their depiction on a plate was apposite, as information was regarded as 'food for the mind'. Kobyletskaya graduated from the Drawing School in Petersburg in 1910, specialising in painting on ceramics and china. Worked at ceramic factories in Denmark, Sweden and France. Worked at the Imperial porcelain factory between 1912–1914, then again 1918–1923. Created over 1500 designs and sketches, but from 1932 moved to specialise in illustrating botanical publications of the Academy of Sciences of the USSR.

Right Mikhail Mikhailovich Adamovich, *Red Star Plate,* 1920. Cobalt blue border with agricultural and architectural tools, and fishnet containing a fish. Border motifs in polished and matt gold. The cavetto displays the Adamovich trademark, a red star containing a hand plough and hammer, also shows the monogram of the new republic RSFSR in Cyrillic letters.

Adamovich graduated for the Stroganov School of Art and Industrial Design in Moscow, then went to Italy to study decorative art from 1907– 1909. On his return he worked on paintings for the interiors of buildings in Moscow and St Petersburg. He also worked in Greece, commissioned by the Greek government to produce a mosaic for the tomb of King George I. Worked for the State Porcelain Factory 1918–1919 before a spell in the Red Army. Returning to the Factory, his time in the army can be clearly seen to influence his later work. Worked at other porcelain factories before returning to do more paintings in buildings in Moscow from 1934–1947.

Right Natan Isaevich Altman, *The Land is for the Workers,* Plate, 1919. Photo Courtesy of Christies' Images Ltd 1999.

Altman was a painter, graphic artist and theatre designer. Studied at art school in Odessa, then in Paris. From 1910 contributed to many avant-garde exhibitions, including '0.10' where Malevich launched Suprematism. Taught at Svomas (free art studios) Petrograd, and was a member of the IZO Narkompros (Visual Arts Section, Commissariat of Enlightenment). Drew portraits of Lenin from life, decorated Uritsky Square Petrograd for the first anniversary of the Revolution, later using a detail as a central motif of this plate. Moved to Paris 1929 to 1935, before returning to Leningrad in 1936. In addition to painting also worked as theatrical designer and book illustrator.

Above Mikhail Mikhailovich Adamovich, *He who does not work does not eat*, 1923. Porcelain plate. Photo Courtesy Christie's Images Ltd 1999.

An adaption of the biblical verse from St Paul's Second Epistle to the Thessalonians, chapter 3 verse 10: 'If any will not work, neither let him eat.' It was incorporated into the constitution of the RSFSR (Russian Soviet Federated Socialist Republic) in 1918. Here it dances around the border of the plate in multi-coloured letters, framing a composition with an image of Lenin (adapted from the famous portrait by Altman), some ration cards, a half an imperial eagle and a red star. 'In the prototype of this plate created in 1921, the red star of the revolution is on top of the eagle, obliterating and crushing it. However, when copies of the plate were ordered, the factory artists were obviously unfamiliar with the symbols and thought it a pity to cover up the eagle, so they painted the star underneath. One often finds such anomalies in agitprop porcelain' (Revolutionary Ceramics, Soviet Propaganda Ware 1917–1927, Nina Lobanov-Rostovsky, Laurence King 1990).

The amazing work produced was varied in content and style, and a number of differing influences, traditions and movements can be identified as informing the painting and designs. References to the thousand-year-old tradition of Russian ikon painting are obvious in a number of artists' work. *Ikon* means image or likeness, the visible and material reflection of things unseen or spiritual, and whilst being objects of worship they were also intended to be read by the onlooker as pictorial commentaries on the scriptures they referred to.

In addition, the *lubok*, folk woodcuts with illustrative texts and subject, which had existed in Russia from the early 17th century, had a formative influence on a number of artists of various backgrounds and schools who worked at the factory. The lubok contained stories, songs and narrative dealing with religion, political and social issues.

Finally, a strong graphic practice developed and flowered for a short while after the Czar's manifesto of 1905 which allowed a limited freedom of the press. Several hundred satirical newspapers and journals sprang up, and the World of Art group of artists (based in St Petersburg) became active contributors. Momentarily forgetful of their group's appeal for pure art, they created angry caricatures and satirical drawings denouncing the oppression of the Czar, his generals and ministers. The later brutal repression reinforced their politicisation, their awareness of the value and social significance of artistic endeavour.

Left Rudolf F. Vilde, Large dish, *In aid of the Famine Stricken Population of the Volga Region*, 1922. Photo courtesy of Sothebys.

In 1920–1921, millions of Russians died from famine and a typhus epidemic. A series of plates and dishes were made by the factory artists for a special sale for the starving population of the Volga region. The sale or auction, in fact, never took place, and the works were the last agitprop works to be made by different artist working in one particular subject. Vilde's painting shows a worker wielding a sledgehammer in his right hand with a rifle in his left, attacking the gloating Grim Reaper who holds a scythe and sheaf of golden corn. Golden Cyrillic letters read 'In aid of the Famine Stricken Population of the Volga Region'. After studying at the Prokhovorov Factory in Moscow, Vilde trained in St Petersburg, and graduated with the title 'expert graphic artist' in 1899. His school funded a scholastic trip to Germany, France and Italy. Worked on interior decoration and decorative art designs for publications. From 1906 to 1938 was head of painting workshop at the State Porcelain factory.

The work produced in the first ten year period in particular was revolutionary in more than one sense of the word. Compared to the now tired, tight, trite, conservative, overworked, and overembellished painting on imperial porcelains, the new works using bold, bright colours, were positively bristling with graphic innovation and design. In addition, the overtly political nature of many of the subjects' commentary on the ceramic surface (which had already had some mileage from Nevers to Staffordshire), was done with such style and panache that one French critic even went so far as to claim that in chinaware 'the revolution has found its highest and clearest expression. Indeed, it would be no exaggeration to claim that they are unique: they provide a document the historical reliability of which cannot be challenged, and they supply, in a masterful artistic form, a record of the mood of the times. Never before or since have contemporary themes in porcelain achieved such political clarity'[27].

In 1923, Chekhonin left the State factory at Petrograd to work at the Volkhov Factory near Novgorod, taking a number of factory artists with him. The Suprematist artist Nicolai Suetin and several others filled the places of those that had left and in 1932, Suetin became art director.

[27] quoted in *Art into Production, Soviet Textiles, Fashion and Ceramics 1917–1935*, Lydia Anreeva, Crafts Council, Ministry of Culture USSR, 1984

Above Conrad Atkinson, *You Can Taste the Third World in a Western Meal*, 1996. Stamped and painted underglaze, on earthenware. The words come from several places in Atkinson's work published in a commission in a page for ARTPAPERS (Atlanta) in 1994:

You can taste the third world in a Western Meal
You can hear the third world in a Western song
You can feel the third world in a Western sculpture
You can smell the third world in a Western perfume
You can eat the third world in a Western restaurant
*   and you can buy the third world in a Western mall.*

Right Paul Scott, *The Accuracy of Artillery Radar, Produce of Israel*, 1996. Inglaze screen printed decal and onglaze decals on bone china plates. Photo Andrew Morris.

More recent use of plates with appropriate political messages. Atkinson's message refers to the use Western companies make of good fertile land in developing countries to provide fruit and vegetables all year round (even when they are out of season) in the wealthy countries of the northern and western hemispheres. This production is often at a not insubstantial cost to the host country which has has to import the industrial agrochemical industries from the West to go with intensive production. In providing food for the West, food production for local consumption is often badly affected as the best land is given over to producing crops for export, and the introduction of modern industrial agricultural practices can lead to significant environmental degradation.

The Accuracy of Artillery Radar, Produce of Israel refers to the shelling of the Cana refugee camp in southern Lebanon by the Israelis in April 1996, killing over 100 women and children. Independent observers concluded that in spite of protestation to the opposite, the Israeli military knew that the camp was full of refugees. Britain imports fruit and vegetables from Israel, and the message on the plate is based on a label from a box of cherry tomatoes bought at a supermarket the day after the bombing. It questions consumer complicity with the oppressive act of a country which produces a significant amount of Britain's imported food.

Top Kazimir Malevich, plate with Suprematist design. Onglaze enamel on porcelain plate. Lomonosov Porcelain Factory Museum, St Petersburg.

Suprematism was an early form of geometric abstraction, avoiding representation of the visible world in favour of 'economic geometry', free from stylistic references. Malevich believed that abstraction also represented the physical embodiment of spirituality. As the artwork was to stand only for itself, as 'pure art', it is perhaps surprising to find it so well used on porcelain plates and forms. However, Malevich regarded the painting *White on White* made in 1918 as the zenith of his exploration of geometric abstraction, and the works on porcelain were made some years later in the early 1920s. The Suprematists regarded white as the ideal support as it expressed weightlessness, so the porcelain's glazed surface was the perfect material. The painted designs (transposed from rectangular paper to the circular ground of a plate) of red, yellow, black and blue triangles, squares, rectangles and circles interact and float across the face of the surface. 'Although the image harmonises content and form, the colour and linear energy of the designs are so overpowering that they visibly invade the borders of the object, giving a sense of universality'[28].

Above Vasilii V. Kandinsky: cup and saucer with pink rims early 1920s. Stroganov School of Art and Industrial Design Moscow. Important painter, who produced designs for a number of works in ceramic medium, including wall tile murals. Later taught at the Bauhaus.

Right Nicolai M. Suetin, plate with orange, black and magenta Suprematist design. Onglaze enamel on porcelain plate. Lomonosov Porcelain Factory Museum, St Petersburg.

[28] quoted in *Art into Production, Soviet Textiles, Fashion and Ceramics 1917–1935*, Lydia Anreeva, Crafts Council, Ministry of Culture USSR, 1984

Only two stores, one in Petrograd and one in Moscow, sold the propaganda porcelain. Elena Danko, an artist at the State Porcelain Factory, creates an impression of the magic that the window displays created. In her memoirs she wrote: 'People who remember the Petrograd of those years, the streets with potholes from missing paving stones, the cold empty houses plunged into darkness, the windows pockmarked with the spidery stars of recent bullet holes, they will also remember the porcelain display window on the Nevsky Prospect. Red stars blazed on shiny white plates, the hammer and sickle flashed in subdued gold, fantastic flowers were interwoven into the RSFSR monogram. You could also see little porcelain Red Guards in the window, and sailors and partisans and chess sets pitting the red guards against the white army. An inscription framed by a garland of flowers on a large white platter proclaimed, "we will transform the world into a flowering garden" '[29].

The revolutionary intention was that ultimately these products would be available to all the masses: 'However, all such high quality wares from the State Porcelain Factory have one constant disadvantage – they are difficult to obtain, since all the original articles are too expensive for the average buyer. This was at any rate the case until recently, though already the situation is beginning to change. The State Porcelain Factory must become an artistic laboratory, creating patterns, whilst other factories of the Central Porcelain Trust which produce inexpensive china must begin to make copies on a vast scale. In addition, thanks to the mechanical china printer recently invented by Chekhonin, it will be possible to produce low-priced articles from the drawings of any major artist, thus bringing beauty and pleasure to the everyday lives of workers' and peasant families' (from an article reviewing the 'Soviet Porcelain' exhibition, 1926, quoted in *Art into Production, Soviet Textiles, Fashion and Ceramics 1917–1935*, Crafts Council, Ministry of Culture USSR, 1984). It never happened. It seldom made it to the homes of ordinary people, and in later years as the priorities of the state turned towards the mass production of cheap functional wares, the imagery, painting and decoration became obsolete to industrial production.

Although the initial revolutionary ardour failed to make the work accessible to the masses, products from the State

Above Romans Suta (1896–1944), *Construction*, 1926. Painting on earthenware, 35.5 cm (14") dia., inv.nr. DLMIK-234. Photo by Maris Kundzins, courtesy Decorative Applied Art Museum, Riga, Latvia.

Porcelain Factory (and others) were used in the RSFSR embassies around the world, and widely exhibited in exhibitions in Europe, in order to generate much needed foreign currency, and to promote the artistic achievements of the Revolution. Their influence can still be seen today in the contemporary ceramic traditions of countries of the former Soviet republics, where ceramic artists have continued, until relatively recently, to work in or alongside factories. Although their material and technological assistance was essential at times, there was also a philosophical acceptance of the value of a relationship between artists and industry, even though it seems that this did not translate into innovative designs and products for industry itself.

Baltars Workshop
In the Latvian Republic, graphic porcelain work of a discernibly different, but related character was produced. A porcelain painting workshop Baltars (Ars Baltica – 'the Baltic art') was founded in 1924. Although a number of fine artists worked there, Romans Suta, Aleksandra Belcova, Sigismunds Vidbergs were the core of

[29] Alexander Lavrin in 'Porcelain for a New World' published in *Where Moscow* March, 1998

the group. For them all, painting on porcelain was a small but significant episode in their differing careers in the visual arts.

It is tempting to view the episode as simply an extension of Soviet Propaganda Ware, but this would be wrong. Latvia was an independent state from 1918–1940 and was not under Soviet political rule. Although Sigismunds Vidbergs had studied in St Petersburg and was clearly influenced by his time there, he was the only one. In addition, unlike the Soviet porcelain, much of which was produced

by artisans copying designs in a factory, the painting and drawings on these pieces were all done by the artists themselves, and the intentions behind most of the work was less overtly political.

During the first two years of Baltars, more than 300 painted porcelain and faience objects (mainly plates, either imported or made in Riga) were produced by artists. The art critic Tatjana Suta (daughter of Romans Suta) defines the painting and drawing style as 'national constructionism' (a terminology based on the artists' own statements).

Other relationships have been identified with Latvian cubism and the obvious, Russian agitprop porcelain. In spite of the aims of the group to sell the plates for profit, this was not easy in Latvia, and although there was some success in international exhibitions, the group finished its work on July 1, 1928. Because of the general economic crisis, it never restarted. (By far the largest collection of Baltars work is in the possession of the Decorative Applied Art Museum in Riga, Latvia.)

53

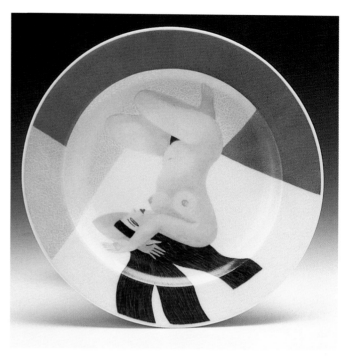

Above left Dalia Lauckaite Jakimaviciene, *A Feast* (Lithuania). 1998 30 cm dia (12").

Above right Inese Brandts, *Dream of Love*, 1998. Onglaze enamel painting on porcelain plate (from Lubiana, Poland), 27 cm (10.5") dia. Photo by Aigars Jukna.

Left Maruta Raude, *Garden with Ladders*, 1998. Onglaze enamel painting on porcelain 32 cm (13") dia. Photo by Aigars Jukna.

Inspired by the Baltars' paintings, Raude started to work on porcelain after studying graphics at the Academy of Arts in Riga. Born, and having grown up in a small town in the countryside, she now lives 'in a concrete blockhouse in Riga'. Her subject matters in recent times have been 'gardens, trees, plants and birds sometimes, a slightly surreal place where one can feel the presence of the human ... some items left by them ... half drunken cups of tea, picked fruits on the table. Garden as a symbol, a paradise garden, as the first garden.'

Right John Everett, *Tea Clipper;* Paul Nash, *Tiger,* designs for Foley, for the 'Exhibition of Contemporary Art for the Table', Harrods, 1935. Courtesy Trustees of the Wedgwood Museum, Barlaston, Staffordshire, England.

Other European movements

The surface was also important to the Italian Futurist ceramic movement Aeroceramica. After seeing Soviet Propaganda porcelain in the Paris exposition in 1925, its founder, Tullio d'Albisola, returned to his father's pottery in Italy and with others produced a manifesto for futurist ceramics. Like the Baltars, one of the motivations of using ceramics was the possibility it seemed to hold out for earning some money, the other was a philosophical belief in making artwork available to the proletariat. There was a notion of producing limited editions of Futurist works in ceramic. In the years between 1928 and 1939, painters, sculptors and poets produced ceramics, exploring the possibilities of form, sculpture, and surface, some with startling brightness and graphic qualities.

Whilst the Baltars and Futurists were not that interested in the industrial use of images on porcelain, factories in other parts of Europe were awakening to the possibilities of using fine artists, and the idea of artists with graphic backgrounds having an input on to the industrial surface.

The Modernist Bauhaus movement attempted to unify the visual arts, design and industry, and although at times it employed people such as Kandinsky and Klee, its eventual rejection of inherently 'decadent' decoration meant that it contributed little to the graphic development of the ceramic surface. Instead it concentrated on the refinement of form, with any decoration subservient to it.

British development

If Soviet Porcelain did influence the British, it was at a very diluted level. The conservative pottery industry never really embraced Modernism either, moving only slowly to

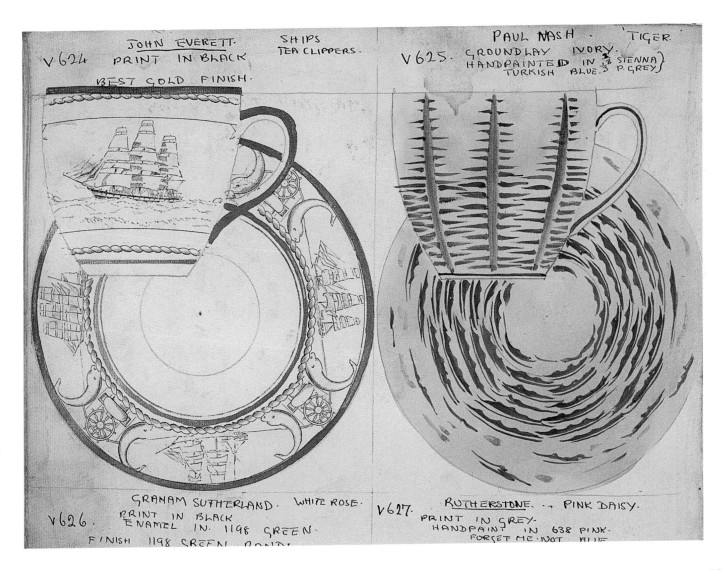

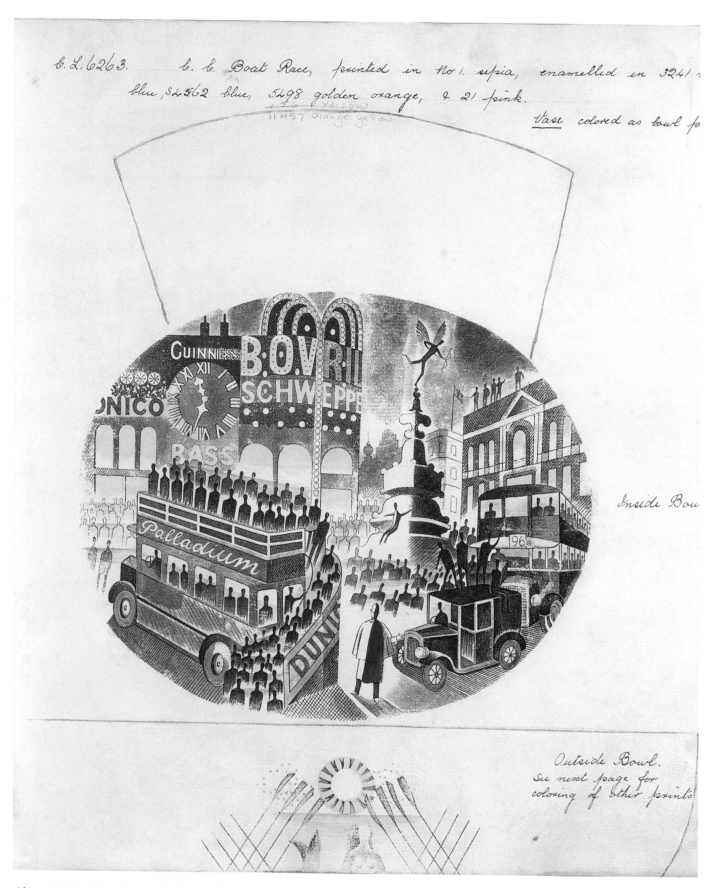

Above Eric Ravilious, Pattern book entry featuring the interior design for the *Boat Race Bowl*, 1938. Courtesy Trustees of the Wedgwood Museum, Barlaston, Staffordshire, England.

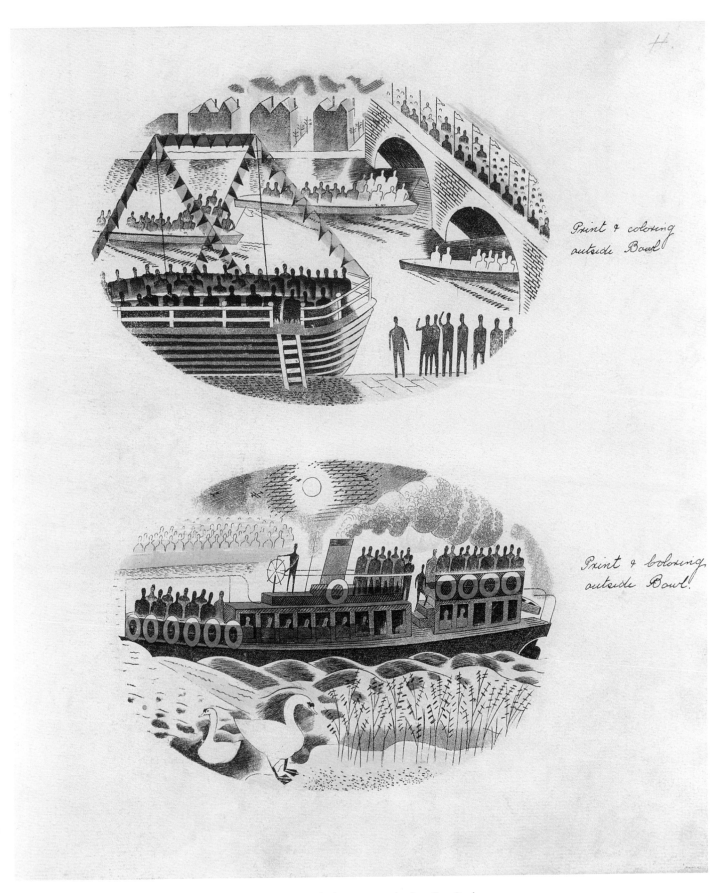

Print & coloring outside Bowl

Print & coloring outside Bowl!

Above Eric Ravilious, Pattern book entry for exterior views which appear on the *Boat Race Bowl*, 1938. Courtesy Trustees of the Wedgwood Museum, Barlaston, Staffordshire, England.

incorporate new ideas and designs. One project that did inject some graphic innovation to the surface of industrial wares was initiated by E. Brain and Co., the Wilkinson Pottery and Foley. Entitled 'An Exhibition of Contemporary Art for the Table', and held at Harrods in London in 1935, it showed work of leading ceramic designers such as Clarice Cliff, and freelance designs for the ceramic surface by high profile painters Paul Nash, Graham Sutherland and Ben Nicholson amongst others.

Josiah Wedgwood V, concerned at the stagnation of surface design, then employed a number of the exhibitors and later Eric Ravilious to produce designs for the Wedgwood Pottery Company. Ceramic painter, Victor Skellern was appointed Art Director. With his longstanding service to Wedgwood, and his links with the Royal College, he knew intimately the possibilities and restrictions of industrial, ceramic graphic production, but had an insight to the preoccupations and perceptions of artists. He acted to facilitate the production of paper designs onto and into the glaze surface, attempting to meld the artistic intent and industrial production together. (An interesting Skellern recollection is detailed in Ravilious and Wedgwood, Richard Dennis 1995: 'When he [Ravilious] first came, and being a very skilled wood engraver, he was most anxious to have one engraver allocated to him with whom he could correspond and train to produce the style of engraving he had in

Above Sigismunds Vidbergs (1890–1970), *Latvija 1918*. 1925. Ink drawing on porcelain plate, 25.5 cm (10") dia. inv.nr. DLM/K-274. Commemorating Latvia's Fight for Independence (or the War of Liberation as it is sometimes called) waged against Russian and German Troops. Photo by Maris Kundzins, courtesy Decorative Applied Art Museum, Riga, Latvia.

Below Clare Leighton, group of plates from the 'New England Industries' series – featuring (left to right) *Logging*, *Gristmilling*, and *Marble Quarrying*, 1952. Courtesy Trustees of the Wedgwood Museum, Barlaston, Staffordshire, England. Clare Leighton designed the 'New England' series in 1952, and demonstrates her skill as an illustrator specialising in woodcuts. The series involved the latest techniques of photo-lithography.

mind. This was a bit of a problem, and might have caused a lot of trouble in the engraving shop, so I persuaded Ravilious to let us cut the first pattern and get his comments. I sent prints to him, and the reply was full of unbounding joy and enthusiasm – this was the engraver he wanted. I had found the right man who knew exactly what he wanted. When he next came to the factory and I had to admit that every one of the engravers – and there were ten of them had each done a separate part of the engraving, he took this very well, and remarked, "I will never argue about the Wedgwood engraving any more, these chaps are without doubt the finest engravers I have ever met!" '

Ravilious' designs were quintessentially English, effectively capturing the tranquillity of life in some parts of England between the wars. The appeal of his line work 'lies in the narrative quality and not in the immediate impact of an abstract motif'[30]. The work was difficult for some pre-war, conservative tastes, and was not an immediate commercial success. Unfortunately, as a war artist, Ravilious was killed in the course of a mission in 1942, and was never to see or appreciate the critical and more commercial suc-

cess of his work that was to follow. In 1952 after the relaxation of war restrictions which allowed only the production of undecorated wares for local consumption, a range of Ravilious products were marketed by Wedgwood with some success.

Wedgwood have continued their erratic tradition of working with artists outside the pottery industry which goes as far back as George Stubbs and John Flaxman. Clare Leighton's work in the 1950s is a good example of strong imagery effectively employed on the ceramic surface, giving a depth and crispness to woodcut imagery quite different to the print produced on paper.

Glenys Barton worked as Artist in Residence at the factory in the 1970s, producing sculptural ceramics with a subtle and highly sophisticated lithographed surface, and Eduardo Paolozzi produced designs for plates in the around the same time. More recently the company has produced a series of plates in limited edition for the National Art

30 Sharon Gater in 'Eric Ravilious, a designer ahead of his time', *Studio Pottery*, No. 24.

Collections Fund. Artists involved included John Piper, Patrick Heron, Patrick Caulfield, Eduardo Paolozzi, Bruce McLean and Peter Blake.

The Royal Worcester factory has also had some close relationships with artists, mainly on the sculptural side, preferring to employ artists and painters on a long term basis, and keeping painting and graphics 'in house'. A notable exception was the employment of Scottie Wilson, an untrained artist with work in the Tate Gallery London, and many other collections. Neal French who worked with him at Worcester describes him as a 'primitive visionary painter' who first painted and drew on secondhand plates bought at Caledonian market London. 'Fascinated by the shininess of the glaze and the cornerless shape of plates and dishes, his small repertoire of continuously repeated themes looked different on them than on the flat matt rectangular card he usually used.' In 1962, at the Ben Uri Gallery, he exhibited his plates, painted with Woolworths enamel, framed and mounted. The Art Director at Royal Worcester, Robert Baker (from the Royal College) invited Wilson to create designs for a screenprint pattern to go on a new earthenware range. Scottie was initially quite at a loss as to how to go about the task, needing the help and

advice of French who guided him through the necessary requirements for a design for screenprinting. 'The designs he did were masterly. He may not have known anything about the mechanics of fitting or screenprinting, but he had an uncanny feel for what would look good on what – frequently the most unexpected device.'

Unfortunately like Ravilious, his designs were a commercial failure, and a polychrome design for porcelain oven/tableware was shelved just as it was to go into production. 'The same paintings on dishes that triggered the whole thing are still there to be admired in galleries, the pity is that they could have been on breakfast tables across the country' (Neal French in 'Scottie Wilson', *Ceramic Review* 98, 1986).

Factory residency programmes

Industrial associations with fine artists have also taken a different form: in the provision of factory space and skills to practising artists in residency programmes. Factories in countries formerly under Soviet economic and cultural influences have long been associated with independent artistic production, but the phenomena is also manifest in the USA and Japan. At the Kohler Company in Kohler,

Right Ann Agee (USA), *Tiled Panel with Workers Portraits in the Kohler Company Pottery.* Underglaze blue on earthenware tiles, 3 m x 6.01 m (10' x 20'), 1991.

Left Scottie Wilson, *Painting on Plate.* Woolworth enamels painted on Johnson Bros earthenware coupe dish, early 1960s. 36 cm x 28 cm (14" x 11"). Photo courtesy of Neil French.

60

Wisconsin, the sanitary ware company which produces thousands of toilets, bathtubs and sinks every day, an artist is usually at work alongside the 3,000 blue collar workforce. Organised by the John Michael Kohler Arts Foundation, the residency programme has been in existence for over 25 years. 'At first the workforce employees were very sceptical says Ruth Kohler, the programmes creator, and a member of the company's founding family. They had a stereotypical view of artists as flaky and not necessarily having the skills the factory people had. Over the years however the workers and the artists began to appreciate each other's craft. For the artists the factory is rich in creative possibilities'[31].

Whilst many artists choose to work in the foundry, or with the production of ceramic forms and sculptural works, Ann Agee's work has been concerned entirely with painting. Trained as a painter, she became 'unattracted to the sacredness of the rectangle'[32] and started to paint and work in ceramics. In her first residency at Kohler she began by sketching the Kohler employees, whilst exploring the possibilities of making teapots. The teapot project soon

became a matter of little interest, and she began to paint with delft blue on tiles, toilets, urinals, bidets, sinks, and water fountains. A mural featuring the likenesses of 25 pottery workers, a series of 40 cm (16") portrait platters, two murals of surrounding Sheboygan County, five bathroom fixtures, and wall tiles depicting bathroom related vignettes were some of the products of her first residency.

The work is narrative, documenting as it does the lives and aspirations of the factory workers. 'The platters tell the stories of a struggling farmer who works two jobs and 20 hour days, a divorced man and his two sons, a worker who laminated Princess Diana's picture to the inside of another worker's pass, a secretary who raises golden retrievers, a former prisoner whose life is revealed in jailhouse tattoos and so on.'[33]

In her most recent work, Agee has created a painted Men's Restroom at the new John Michael Kohler Arts Center.

[31] Cynthia Crossen in the *Wall Street Journal*, May 22 1991
[32] Quoted in 'Private Functions/Public Art', *American Craft*, June/July 1993
[33] Anne Agee quoted in 'Art in a Factory', in *Ceramics Monthly*, October 1992

Although injecting new ways of looking and developing the ceramic surface, the relationship of independently thinking painters and graphic artists to the ceramics industry appears to be fraught with problems on a purely commercial level, and it is probably always going to be thus. Experience has suggested to industry that, in direct economic terms, artists are useful only in small doses. Indirectly they are of value, but in a less active role than in the mechanics of industrial production: prestige and status can be conferred to a company by association with an artist's name, and the perception of a company as a benefactor of the arts. Kohler has demonstrated that the latter approach has been a fruitful one for them as well as the artists involved.

Left and below left Ann Agee, detail, Painted Men's Restroom, John Michael Kohler Arts Centre, Sheboygan, Wisconsin 1998. Painted tiles and fixtures, dimensions variable. Photo courtesy of John Michael Kohler Arts Centre.

Above Charlotte Hodes, dish, 32 cm x 41 cm (12.5" x 16"), 1997, collaged slide on transfers and tissue copperplate engravings with painted onglaze colour.

In 1997, painter Charlotte Hodes was commissioned by the City Museum and Art Gallery, Stoke-on-Trent to make a series of monumental paintings which explored the relationship of the figure within a decorative framework. As a result of the solo exhibition, she was invited to work at the Spode factory. She had complete freedom to use their forms and had access to their considerable library of transfers, copperplate engravings and pattern books.

'The work that I produced there was very much a response to this extensive and extraordinary archive dating back 200 years. These are both part of the Spode Museum and of the factory itself. I was particularly interested to use this archive as a protagonist, juxtaposing and collaging my own visual material to make images which could play with the past whilst celebrating the present. The aesthetic of the Spode tradition emerged out of the interpretation of something that already existed, that is, the ceramics and designs from China. My particular interest in working at Spode was that I in turn was re-interpreting their own interpretations and assimilations' (Charlotte Hodes 1998).

CHAPTER 4

Clay Visitors:
Chagall, Cocteau, Cubism,
CoBrA, and Co. —
and Duchamp

Dr Roland Doschka, writing in the introduction to *Terra Sculptura, Terra Pictura*, Museum Het Kruithuis, s'Hertogenbosch 1992) observes: 'From antiquity to the renaissance universality was quite a common phenomenon. Most artists are at the same time sculptors, painters and occasionally even architects. But ever since the 17th century a painter is a painter, a sculptor is a sculptor.'

Until recently, most books, collections and exhibitions have reinforced this monochromatic view of the artist (indeed a painter is a painter of fresco or oils, but not the ceramic). Referencing mainstream books and exhibitions on featuring European painters, one could be forgiven for thinking that a brushful of glaze had never found its way into a painter's hand. In reality, artists have used ceramic materials to paint with at various times since the 17th century (see Chapter 3, George Stubbs and paintings at Zsolnay). With the breaking down of traditional perceptions and definitions of art towards the end of the 19th century, there were an increasing, and significant, number who began to explore the ceramic surface.

The Soviet and the Latvian Baltars experiments with fine artists working graphically on industrial porcelain were high profile manifestations of this. Later in Britain Sam Haile and Bob Washington were to translate surrealism into the ceramic surface in between the two world

Wars. The CoBrA group of artists in Continental Europe lurched off in a direction of their own, and in Australia, Arthur Boyd and others were to explore in some depth the painting potential of the medium.

Perhaps the most significant appropriation of ceramic materials by painters began before any of these. Running alongside industrial pottery production facilities in Europe, the folk and craft tradition of handmade pottery was still very much alive in rural areas of France. Here, small workshops used locally sourced ceramic materials to produce distinctively regional pottery products. It was within this genre that Gauguin, Miró, Matisse, Braque, Chagall, Cocteau, Dufy and Picasso began to use clay, the raw material; all for painting and drawing, and some also used it for sculptural explorations too.

Their investigations of the sculptural possibilities of clay were not clouded by some deep philosophical necessity to involve the form and function of clay objects, rather they were the natural physical enquiries of visually active brains (clay does that, it invites manipulation).

Others were more interested to explore the aesthetic possibilities of mark making, painting, and drawing with clay, glaze and ceramic pigments. They all discovered the transforming effect of fire on clay and glazed surface, producing deeply intense, glassy colours, so different to oil on

canvas, and so unpredictable. For these the three dimensional possibility of ceramics was not necessarily a factor in the equation. This work, like the agitporcelain and Baltars, has not endeared them to the Craft establishment (in the UK at least), who view such incursions as superficial. In reality the work threatens the philosophical base of the 'Craft' claim to a disputed area of visual art activity, and it is this that makes the work dangerous for them.

Chaplet, Metthey and Artigas

Gauguin was first introduced to ceramist Ernest Chaplet in 1886. Chaplet had apprenticed at Sevres, but by now was producing hand thrown stoneware. His studio was near Gauguin's residence in Paris, and soon the painter began

Above József Rippl-Rónai (Hungary): *Woman's Portrait*, 1898. Chrome pencil drawing on pyrogranit 47 cm x 64 cm (18.5" x 25"). Made at Zsolnay Factory Pécs, Hungary. Zsolnay, Janus Pannonius Múzeum, Pécs, Hungary. Photo by István Füzi.

The Hungarian painter József Rippl-Rónai studied in Paris in the late 1880s, coming into contact with the Nabis, who had close links with Toulouse - Lautrec. He developed his own style of Art Nouveau, and was deeply influenced by Symbolist painting. He eventually returned to Hungary, living not far from the city of Pécs, which houses the famous Zsolnay ceramics factory. He undertook a number of works in ceramic at the Factory in the late 1890s. Lautrec was experimenting with differing methods of drawing, including thinned oils on cardboard and lithography, and Rippl-Rónai's ceramic drawings can be seen as another manifestation of the exploratory mood of the time.

working with this 'perfect medium for expressing his love of raw materials and his decorative sense'. His work was almost exclusively sculptural, but several forms were receptors for painted and incised imagery, often of the motifs common to his Breton paintings. 'For Gauguin, the art of pottery was inextricably linked with that of painting. The Brittany sketchbooks show numerous motifs common to his paintings as well as many design for ceramics. The evolution of his ceramic oeuvre is part of Gauguin's general stylistic development toward an increasing complex symbolism.' [34]

Ten years later, the Hungarian painter József Rippl-Rónai after a spell in Paris was to work on large stoneware tiles, drawing with chrome oxide crayons.

Ceramist, André Metthey, opened a studio in Asnières on the banks of the Seine in Paris in 1901. Metthey began experimenting with on or inglaze colours on tin glaze, in the manner of delft or maiolica, producing bright intense coloured glazed surfaces. A number of the Fauvists including Bonnard, Derain, Vuillard, Redon, Maurice de Vlaminck and Henri Matisse worked with him from 1906 to 1909 painting earthenware. The Fauvists were interested in strong pure colours, and flat pattern, and the evidence is that they discovered a bright and intense palette, but in another medium. Ambroise Vollard is credited with instigating the co-operative venture [35] and the results of the collaboration were admired in the Salon d'Automne in 1907.

Following the First World War, Catalan painter and ceramist Llorens Artigas moved from Barcelona to Paris where from 1923 to 1941 he too collaborated with a number of painters. These included Joan Miró, Raoul Dufy and

[34] Claire Frèches-Thory, quoted in 'Gauguin's Ceramics', in *Ceramics Monthly*, October 1989
[35] Dr Hans-Jörgen Heuser in 'Französische Keramik zwischen 1850–1910', quoted in *Terra Sculptura, Terra Pictura*, Museum Het Kruithuis, s'Hertogenbosch 1992

Left De Vlaminck, *Untitled*, plate 10" x 15" (25 x 38 cm). Collection Museum Het Kruithuis:

'The plate is merely a tondo for his painting of a fluttering bird spreading its wings. The closest thing to an acknowledgment of the plate form is a double band decoration on the rim. The bands frame the image like the frame around any canvas does.' He uses 'the kind of sinuous organic line that has been combined happily with the curves of ceramic forms since the beginning of time . . . it has a fluid brushiness that almost seems like watercolour,' Janet Koplos in The Unexpected, Artist Ceramics of the Twentieth Century, *Museum Het Kruithuis, s'Hertogenbosch, Harry N. Adams Inc, 1998.*

Above Raoul Dufy, *Nu Accoude,* 1925. Tile 15.5 x 15.5 cm (6" x 6"). Collection Museum Het Kruithuis. Tiles are ultimately as receptive to paintings as paper and canvas, they are flat, not even the rim of a plate or a light concavity to distract.

67

Albert Marquet. Raoul Dufy's brother Jean, was also a painter and watercolourist and painted porcelain for Haviland and Cie at Limoges, and later worked at Sèvres. From 1922 to 1930 Raoul collaborated with Artigas, painting and drawing on pots, architectural forms and tiles. In the mid-1920s he too began designing for Sèvres, a reflection of his wide interests in the applied arts (he also produced designs for textiles and worked with couturier Paul Poiret).

One thing that is never discussed in the accounts of the 'visitors' is that the process of painting on biscuit ceramic or dry glazed surface is quite different to paper or canvas. For the Fauvists working on tin glaze there would have been no time to go back and correct; the dry glaze sucks the water from the pigment as soon as the brush passes over the surface, and the paint is dry. Not like the watercolourist who can go back to work and flood the paper with water, nor like oil paint which maintains its tactile tackiness for a time; the painted stroke of ceramic pigment is dry before the brush completes its sweep. It forces positive confident brush marks and a style of painting evolves that takes account of these material properties.

Above right Raoul Dufy, *Jardin des Papillons*, 1926–1927. Object 26 x 23 x 42 cm (10 x 9 x 16"). Collection Museum Het Kruithuis.

An 'apartment garden', made by Artigas and painted by Dufy. 'Not content with simple sculptural suggestiveness, Dufy has fantastically painted the walls of the courtyard and the house itself. Some of the depictions set the scene of this place: fountain, water, sailing ships. But the piece gets its name from his proportionately enormous renderings of butterflies' (Janet Koplos in The Unexpected, Artist Ceramics of the Twentieth Century, *Museum Het Kruithuis, s'Hertogenbosch, Harry N. Abrams Inc. 1998).*

For the painter this process is an inherently pleasurable one, and Dufy's style is so suited to it. It is no wonder that he persisted with his painting on clay for so long.

Artigas was also to work with Joan Miró over a long period. Miró's intention in working with the ceramic was not simply to apply glaze and colour to clay as if it were simply another white canvas, there were altogether more ambitious ideas behind the work. 'Before I actually carried out any pottery, I began by painting direct on huge rocks; I wanted to make myself familiar with the elements of the landscape, by putting my stamp on them. I worked in a monumental spirit, thinking of combining my results with architecture. This would be a possible way of ennobling mass-produced buildings and ceasing to treat the people who have to live in them as unfeeling robots'. [36]

[36] *Miró*, Walter Erben, Taschen 1992.

Right Joan Miró: *Tête Carrée*, 1955–56. Object, 30 cm x 30 cm (12" x 12") Collection. Museum Het Kruithuis.

Below Joan Miró, *The Sun, Le Mur du Soleil*, 3m x 15 m 1955–1958, UNESCO Building, Paris. Photo courtesy of Luciphore/UNESCO.

Miró produced a number of large-scale artworks on tiles including pieces for Barcelona Airport, Harvard University and this for the UNESCO building in Paris. He chose a 'brutally dynamic graphism' to achieve a distinctive contrast to surrounding areas of concrete. The first tiles made were found to be unsatisfactory on firing, so a second batch of irregularly shaped tiles similar to old stones in a wall were made. Much to Artigas amazement, Miró painted shapes up to 20 feet (6.1 m) long with a long palm fibre besom dipped in glaze. Received the Grand Award of the Guggenheim Foundation in 1959 for the UNESCO work.

Above Marc Chagall, *Femme Au Coq*, 1962, plate 24.5 cm (9" approx.).
Collection Museum Het Kruithuis.

Chagall's ceramics, like his paintings, are much more dream like and nebulous. Here he drew and modelled the soft clay surface, and in the application of colour and glaze, painted with a fluid, but also tentative way. He knew that the effect of fire and heat was unpredictable, and wanted to exploit that element of the unknown.

'I wanted to feel this earth just like the craftsmen did before and within the borders of the ceramic work I wanted to blow in it the echo of an art at the same time distant and close.' (Quoted in Terra Pictura, Terra Sculptura Museum Het Kruithuis, 1992.) Unlike Picasso and others he did not allow any editioning of his works, but his methodology made that a virtual impossibility anyway. Chagall, worked variously at Madoura, Antibes and Venice.

Right Pablo Picasso, *Still Life with Cherries*, 36 x 58 cm (14" x 23").
Photo courtesy of Images modernes.

White earthenware slab, incised, painted with slips and oxides, partly glazed. A mixture of simple drawing directly in the soft clay surface with bold splashes of colour and brush marks. One of a series of painted and drawn tiles that seem as if they were simply sliced from the block of clay with a wire.

70

On a practical level, Miró's involvement with clay was comprehensive, working on tiles, vessel forms, and sculptural pieces. He modelled idol-like figures, half animal, half fruit, added relief details to forms and tiles, and experimented with firing, painted colours and glazes. He exhibited works made with Artigas in Paris, New York and Barcelona.

Walter Erben asserts that his work in the ceramic was influential in his paintings on canvas: 'From all these experiments Miró acquired knowledge and experience which in turn manifested themselves in his painting and drawing. Alongside lineations of an abstract character appeared others that make no attempt to conceal their origin in modelling. Henceforward we also find in his canvases constellations of colours that show resemblance to the colour effects Miró discovered and studied in connection and mingled with one another: modelling was enriched by colour and line, without losing its characteristic quality; the picture gained by the introduction of forms of expression that had come to Miró through his work in modelling and pottery.'[37]

Miró's large-scale ceramics make clear reference to southern European and Arabic traditions of large-scale tile cladding and artworks, but in inserting his modern and contemporary aesthetic created a monumental leap for the genre. He continued to work with ceramics until the late 1970s.

Other large tiled pieces were produced by Matisse and Chagall. Matisse had been amongst the group first experimenting with painted clay in 1907. He came back to the medium in the late 1940s and produced the commissioned work: La Chapelle de Vence made at the workshop of Jacques Bordillon in Aubagne. He also worked at the Madoura Workshop not far away in Vallauris in 1948, producing several plates with black graphics depicting the head of a woman, or flowers. He was, however, unhappy with the fired results, and apparently broke most of them, and today only three of the ten plates survive. (One in the International Ceramics Museum Faenza, another in the Hermitage, St Petersburg. The other is in a private collection.)

[37] *Miró*, Walter Erben, Taschen 1992.

Vallauris

After exploratory trips in 1946, Vallauris's other most famous resident, Pablo Picasso, moved there in 1948. He had already worked with clay many years before; the Kahnweiller collection contains a female mask dated 1908 and two vases with Picasso and Jean Van Dongen signatures. At some stage, he is also said to have shown 20 ceramic pieces to Artigas, who apparently considered them mediocre; the story goes that Picasso promptly destroyed them. However, here in Vallauris it appears that he was rather more tolerant of his own production, for at least 4,000 surviving ceramic pieces have been attributed to him. He was one of a number of artists (many of whom were attracted there by his presence) who worked in the village over the next 20 years.

Following the Second World War, the previously depressed state of the traditional functional ceramics economy was for a time alleviated by the lack of metals used in the manufacture of cooking vessels. Vallauris had produced utilitarian and architectural ceramics since Roman times, and young makers and designers, committed to traditional values, but promoting modern design moved into the village to set up businesses or take over run down factories. The Madoura workshop run by Suzanne and Georges Ramié was one of these.

The renewal in Vallauris was a local manifestation of a wider craft revival in France. Together with pottery's claim to be the most ancient of the arts, its alchemic properties and the purely sensual (which is a seduction that has claimed many) combined in irresistible appeal to Picasso. To refer to him as a 'visitor' to clay is actually misleading, for to consistently work in a material for over 20 years and produce the range of pieces Picasso did, means that he was not a visitor but a master of the genre. He developed a comprehensive assortment of skills in the sculptural formation of raw clay, the graphic adaption of mark, glaze and oxide for painterly ends and the use of plaster moulds to produce editioned ceramic prints: 'With the new material came a resurgence of inspiration and energy that broke new ground and opened up new perspectives across the whole of his work . . . He used and subverted this ancient tradition: a plate becomes a painting, a pot becomes a face, a newspaper a tray, a plate a plate. Also in a culture that tended more and more towards abstraction, he was able to sustain his faith in the art of palette and brush, to which he returned at the end of his life; this was his first and last material and, above all, the chosen weapon of his mind'[38]. But France was not the only place where artists were engaging in ceramics.

38 Bernard Ruiz-Picasso, in *Picasso, Painter and Sculptor in Clay*, Royal Academy of Arts 1998, photo Images Modernes.

Left Pablo Picasso, *Bullfight Scene*, 20/4/51, 29 x 65.5 cm (11½" x 26"). Press moulded Louis XV oval platter, white earthenware painted with oxides, crackled glaze ground.

Bullfighting was long a passion for Picasso, and although Vallauris had no ring itself, he helped finance a temporary one in the summer of his last but one birthday party. He even promoted the corrida with his own lithographic posters: 'bulls were brought and killed breaking every local bylaw in the book. It was the first and last time' (Max Borka, 'Picasso and the Picassiettes' in The Unexpected, Artists' Ceramics of the Twentieth Century, *Museum Het Kruithuis, s'Hertogenbosch, Harry N. Abrams Inc. 1998). The form of the plate is used to convey an impression of the whole event with the central drama played out on the light of the flat centre of the plate, the sides painted to represent the crowd, and the arches of the traditional ring.*

Above Pablo Picasso, *Picador* or *El Picador*. Tiles, 1960, 15.2 x 15.2 cm (6" x 6"). Collection Museum Het Kruithuis.

Above Fernand Léger, *La Pomme Jaune* 1951, relief, 28.5 x 25.5 cm (11" x 10"). Collection Museum Het Kruithuis.

Léger was one of the first Cubists to experiment with non-figurative abstraction. His ceramics are consistent with his previous output, abstracted and innovative. Historically, clay has offered this possibility and Léger exploited it deftly. This shiny still life of brightly coloured yellow, red, blue and green on a bold white form, is boldly delineated in black. There is a sort of double take, the feeling that there is when a print isn't quite registered ... but this illusion is the creation of a surface which is not flat but in relief. Some drawn lines and shapes appear somehow to have moved outwards from the background. He makes no attempt to resurrect or redesign the plate, but instead takes the relief, and removes it from its frame or background so that the image is just that. A halfway stage between a picture and a freestanding form. 'His use of bright colour has always called for an extensive use of white, and his whites have had a tendency to age. Fastened in ceramic, these whites and the colours that play against them are certain to resist the effects of time and unchangingly proclaim his joy in the physical world and his unquenchable optimism' (Otis Gage quoted in The Unexpected, Artists' Ceramics of the Twentieth Century, *Museum Het Kruithuis, s'Hertogenbosch, Harry N. Abrams Inc. 1998). Léger worked at the Ateliers du Tapis Vert in Vallauris, he later founded a ceramics studio at Biot, which in 1957 became the Léger Museum.*

Left Georges Braque, *l'Oiseau Blanc*, 1960, 26.5 cm (10 ½"), edition. Collection Museum Het Kruithuis.

With Picasso, Braque was responsible for the Cubist movement, but his later works were more classically influenced. This design was devised in 1949, and reproduced in a limited edition plate in 1960. The use of a circular ground instead of the painter's usual rectangular or square, proposes different compositional constraints and possibilities. It is something that artists have consistently found of interest and fascination in working on plates. On Braque's platter, the blue does not extend to cover the rim of the white plate. 'The result is a strangely contradictory one: the bird seems more ethereal, more a flight of insubstantial imagination or memory because of the hesitant, fragmentary nature of this background.' (Janet Koplos in The Unexpected, Artists' Ceramics of the Twentieth Century, *Museum Het Kruithuis, s'Hertogenbosch, Harry N. Abrams Inc. 1998.)*

Right Jean Cocteau, *Jeune Fille Florentine*, 1957, 30 cm (12"), ed 22/25. Collection Museum Het Kruithuis.

Cocteau is one of those not known for any sculptural pretensions. He did paint a number of jugs and vases, but his graphic style transferred most naturally to the plate, where the simplicity and virtual flatness of the form place few constraints (apart from the circular) on the drawing. Instead of exploiting the nuance of fired glassy colours, his fresh bold image is created in flat colours and drawn lines. The design is made with respect to the circular form; the shape informs the design. Jean Cocteau worked at the Ateleirs du Tapis Vert in Vallauris.

Below Pablo Picasso, *Head of a Faun*, 8/2/49, 32 x 38 cm (12 ½" x 15"). Press moulded plate, white earthenware, painted with oxides and slips, partly glazed. Private collection. Image courtesy of Images Modernes, Paris.

An image with qualities that could only be created with the use of ceramic materials. The bleeding of metal oxide colour in the glaze is produced when the heat of the kiln causes the glassy frit to melt. Some ceramic palettes have to be learnt by experience, for unfired pigments in oxide form bear little relation to their finished state. The plate as canvas.

Right Asger Jorn: *Untitled*, plate 30 x 39 cm (12" x 15 ½"). Collection Museum Het Kruithuis.

Asger Jorn had friends who were ceramists, working in the studio of Danish potter Niels Nielsen as early as 1933. From 1953 onwards he produced a significant body of works in ceramic including sculptural as well as painterly pieces on plates and large ceramic murals. In 1953 he worked extensively in Silkeborg and Sorring in Jutland's pottery centre.

It was his intention to breathe new life into the area, as Picasso was perceived to have done in Vallauris. 'As his sense of liberation increased, he began to combine layers of clay (engobes) with the glazes, and to work the surface of his products by scraping, moulding and scratching it.' From 1954 his paintings and lithographs informed much of his ceramics, and vice-versa. Produced a huge relief panel (3 m x 27 m) in Albisola for Aarhus Grammar School in Jutland in 1959. Settled in Italy in Albisola, where his house was declared a museum in 1974.

CoBrA

Further North, a group of painters formed the CoBrA group. Named after the cities of Copenhagen, Brussells and Amsterdam, this group of Danish, Belgian, and Dutch artists put their name to a founding manifesto in 1948. Inspired in part by the Picasso/Miró adventure they set off into a ceramic adventure, in a direction all of their own. Like the English potter, Bernard Leach whose admiration for the arts and crafts movement produced work of a completely different nature, the CoBrA artists were also attracted to the ideas of Ruskin and Morris. Their enemy though was not so much industrial toil and lack of soul, but the straitjacket of academic convention in Western Art.

Their desire to practise 'all branches of art' reflected a contemporary philosophical notion that had seen both the Fauvists and the German Expressionist group Die Brücke's involvement in areas of the 'applied arts'. The basic tenet of the CoBrA group was the liberation of individual creativity through free expression. They sought to free themselves from rational Western culture and 'sought a spontaneous expressionistic, anti-classic art which would return to the primordial sources of creation'[39]. They sought inspiration from naive art, children's art, and the art of the mentally ill.

[39] Frederick J. Cummings, quoted in *The Unexpected, Artists' Ceramics of the Twentieth Century*, Museum Het Kruithuis, s'Hertogenbosch, Harry N. Abrams Inc. 1998

Above Karel Appel, *Untitled*, 1953, plate 8 ¼" (21 cm). Collection Museum Het Kruithuis.

In Autumn 1948 just before the formation of CoBrA, painters Appel, Constant, Corneille and Rooskens set up the 'Experimentele Groep in Holland'. They were given the opportunity to work together at the Russel-Tiglia ceramic factory in Teglen that autumn; some subsequently worked individually at times over the following six years. Primarily, they painted plates that were made for them in the factory, and included the imaginary figures that so characterised CoBrA work in other media.

Right Lucebert, *Children of the Sun*, 1950. Collection Museum Het Kruithuis.

Lucebert came to CoBrA as a poet, but later was to be known equally as a painter and draftsman. His involvement in CoBrA stimulated his experimental poetry in the group Vijtigers which sought a similar freedom in language comparable to CoBrA's spontaneity in painting. His paintings in ceramic initially presented figures and animals with mythological themes.

The movement existed for three years, 1948 to 1951, but although not formally in existence after that, the individuals involved continued to produce work which evolved from the childlike, to works with a darker, more brutal feel.

In 1954, the intellectual and driving force behind CoBrA, Danish artist Asger Jorn, in a reaction against the Swiss architect Max Bill's indifference to the 'free arts', formed a new group, the Bauhaus of the Imagination (Movement International pour un Bauhaus Imaginiste, MIBI). The formation of this new group initiated a dialogue between Jorn, and Italian artists, and later Jorn was to move to Albisola, not far from Genoa, the home of the earlier Futurist movement. The physical manifestations of MIBI were two ceramics events that took place over the next summers involving Italians, and artists from the Netherlands, Belgium, France, and Canada, and the body of ceramic work produced as a result. The work demonstrated exuberance and freedom in clay, glaze and colour, and was exhibited at the factory of Tullio Mazotti (also referred to as Tullio d'Albisola) the host of the events. It was a mixture of sculptural and painterly pieces.

The final act of MIBI was to initiate a retrospective of Futurist ceramics held in 1956 at Alba, further inland. Like many events, associations and movements in 20th century art, the seemingly irreconcilable came bundled together: Futurist ceramics with a preference for machine-aesthetics, and fascist overtones (at least towards the end of the movement), with MIBI, overtly exposing Marxist ideals, and the individual expression of personal creativity.

CoBrA artists have continued to work in ceramics.

Boyd

Distanced a little from the politics of art and war in Western Europe, for an influential group of Australian artists in the Melbourne area, clay and glaze became an important part of their creative practice.

Merric Boyd, credited as 'the potter who gave the strongest expression to the Australian romantic bush myth' had an established pottery at Murrumbeena by the early 1920s. With strongly religious feelings, and a passionate sensitivity to the natural environment, he had a background in painting and agriculture, and produced idiosyncratic and individual pottery. He realised 'the two alternative potentials of Art Nouveau linearism – the expressionist and the abstractionist – so he too, seems to have understood, even anticipate the two strands of post-World War II Australian painting – the sensuous enjoyment of the landscape for itself and the revival of the pre-Heidelberg colonial view of the terrible antipodean world. Within this latter tradition it is the more personal and allegorical work – in both paint and clay – of his own immediate circle that the full measure of the importance of Merric Boyd's mystical expressionism is to be found' [40].

By the 1950s Merric Boyd, in spite of an established reputation, had few followers; his ceramics became victim of the fashion for the 'craft' aesthetic fostered by the ideas of Bernard Leach, which had burrowed its way into Australian ceramics as it had in other parts of the Anglicised world. However, Merric's son, painter Arthur Boyd, was able to draw on his family experience of ceramics and decoration to move the ceramic surface into the realm of the serious painter, out of the way of studio pottery.

In 1937 Arthur Boyd established a studio in the garden of his parent's house. After the Second World War, he set up a pottery with fellow painter John Perceval, with a view to supplying domestic wares for sale to subsidise their painting activities. With no formal pottery training, the pair gradually began realise the expressive possibilities the medium offered and began to make ambitious pieces, exuberantly painted in underglaze with mythological and religious imagery.

The pottery, like Madoura, became a centre for other artists, who stopped by to paint a pot or two, others staying on for longer periods producing work that was all their own, forms and all. In 1948, Perceval exhibited paintings and ceramics together, the latter already affecting his work on canvas. Unhappy with the reception of his paintings, he abandoned them for work in ceramic for a number of years, later delighting in the effects of colours and glazes for their own sake.

Arthur Boyd (who went on to be a seminal figure in post-war Australian painting) in contrast had used the surface of pots as a ground for pictures, 'seeming to ignore its three dimensional form'. From 1949 to 1952 and then later in the 1960s, he produced a series of paintings on large tiles. Many on Biblical themes, they relate directly to subjects and compositions also done on canvas.

He worked as a painter, not a decorator, and critically, the methodology used to create these works was innovative. He created a unique palette to paint with using oxides and slips mixed to the consistency of oil paint, later finishing with a deep lead glaze. 'The painting was done with ordinary artists' bristle brushes . . . Cutting into the tile was also done then. While still in its soft state, a coating (a mixture of half tin and half body) was painted over the entire surface. This gave a whiter ground which helped to give a brilliance to colours. Lead glaze was . . . shaken evenly over the tile up to a thick consistency of more than the depth of a matchhead' (Arthur Boyd quoted in *Arthur Boyd, Retrospective*, Art Gallery New South Wales 1994). The outstanding quality of the paintings in ceramic is not a three-dimensional quality, these are paintings on a basically flat ground; the materials impart a different (ceramic) dimension with depth and brilliant glassy colour frequently likened to stained glass.

[40] Quoted in *Australian Studio Pottery and China Painting*, Peter Timms, Oxford University Press 1986

Left Arthur Boyd (Australia), *Lovers in an Orchard*. Ceramic painting, 51.5 x 55.5 cm (20 ½ " x 22"), 1962–1964. Private collection, Sydney. Photo courtesy Art Gallery New South Wales.

Produced in London, these later tiled paintings move away from the dark themes of the earlier work, and are more 'lyrical and fluid'. Lovers in an Orchard was a reworking of a recurrent theme in Boyd's painting of lovers embracing under a flowering tree 'and epitomises the transformation of originally apocalyptic images into lyrical evocations of the pleasure of human love' (Arthur Boyd, *Retrospective*, Art Gallery New South Wales 1994).

Above Arthur Boyd (Australia), *Adam and Eve*. Ceramic painting, 39 cm x 42 cm (15 ½ " x 16 ½ "), 1950–1951. Private collection, Melbourne. Photo courtesy Art Gallery New South Wales.

Boyd claimed no particular commitment to religious faith and his depictions of biblical and mythological events examine the existence of human suffering, weaknesses and corruptibility, in a manner 'hardly reeking with reverence' (quoted in Arthur Boyd, *Retrospective*, Art Gallery New South Wales 1994).

Picasso has rightly been extolled for exploring clay with more of a sculptor's mind than most fine art painters have done. Leopold Foulem sums up the appeal his ceramics have to the world of studio pottery in explaining his use of volume and form: 'Picasso was a sculptor and understood the generic classification underlying ceramics, translated this concept of volume as very few, if any, mainstream artists have at anytime during the past hundred years.' However, Foulem writing about Chagall and Miró's ceramic murals insists 'they are flat surfaces, the imagery is close or similar to these artists pictorialism. . . . true 'ceramicness' is almost nonexistent' (Leopold Foulem in *NCECA Journal*, Vol. 8 Issue 1).

This is to claim that a key element of 'ceramicness' is 'form' or 'volume', and whilst this view has some credence, it seems to ignore the unique qualities generated on the ceramic surface in the kiln, and which can be deployed on surfaces that are flat, or in relief or intaglio. The word 'print' means to impress, and what more impressionable material is there than clay? The intaglio image produced in an unglazed terracotta surface from a plaster print, is ultimately exclusively ceramic… paper cannot do this, or mimic these qualities. Painted (and printed) ceramic colour and pigment in a glassy glaze are features of ultimate 'ceramicness' too: Picasso not only added and informed the ceramic by his three-dimensional contributions, but also by his work on the flat, and the 'two and a half dimensions' of his prints from plaster. Léger too explored the possibilities of abstracted relief, another of those 'ceramicy' things, that can move the base outwards from the flat without involving volume and contained space. Chagall, Miró and Boyd demonstrated that the ceramic palette is different to that of the oil painter, it is a palette with an extra depth and vitality formed in the red heat of the kiln.

Finally, moving back once more to the beginning of the century, a quite unrelated, but nevertheless significant, work cannot go unmentioned. Possibly the most significant ceramic object of the century was a urinal. Marcel Duchamp's entry of a signed urinal (signed 'R. Mutt') into an American exhibition of independent artists in 1917 was not only a significant symbol of the changes

which were marking the end of the dominance of the Renaissance view of the arts, but its physical material content has since given infinite succour to those towards the end of the century who see it as a justification for defining (certain) ceramics as fine art, and for raising the status of 'objects' above paintings.

In 1912 Duchamp, Léger and Brancusi visited the Salon de la Locomotion Aérienne; Duchamp is quoted by Léger as saying to Brancusi: 'Painting is finished. What could possibly be more beautiful than this propellor? Tell me could you do that?' In light of this comment and the profound effect his work had on ideas about art, it might be perceived as a strange reference to have in a book about ceramics and painting . . . but although the urinal became art because of Duchamp's action (in submitting the piece to an art exhibition), part of his action was to graphically alter the (ceramic) piece, by adding a signature, thus proclaiming the work as his own. This is not an attempt to make a 'ceramic' claim to ownership of a seminal fine art object (which no longer physically exists), but to point it out as another example of how the graphic alteration of a ceramic surface can be deeply significant.

Duchamp's ideas surrounding the 'ready made' have been significant for many latter day fine artists (including the photographic images of Jeff Koons and Cindy Sherman, see Al(l)ready Made, catalogue, Museum Het Kruithuis 1992), and still have deep resonances in our perceptions of art at the end of the 20th century.

Left Bruce McLean (UK), plate from dinner service, 1987.

'In 1986 I was invited by Douglas Woolf to visit the Fulham Potteries to collaborate with them and to make a number of works. I accepted and proceeded to make and decorate hundreds of plates and large bowls, some of which were fabricated for me and some of which I made myself. I decided that I would only make functional objects, large meat plates, salad bowls, large wine and beer jugs. Whether or not these objects were art was not important. What was important was did they look good containing stuff and would that stuff enhance the experience? If you believe that an experience such as sitting down to an excellent meal with drinks and good friends enjoying conversation can be art, then your plates, jugs, bowls etc. will have played a significant role in that experience. Venice is a great city, a great work. It is sinking. It is being used. It is great art. What craft is, I don't know; it seems to me that something is either art or it is not.' Bruce McLean, in AN, July 1994.

Right Conrad Atkinson (UK/USA), *Mining Culture in Technicolour,* Atlanta College of Art Gallery 1998.

Above and right Conrad Atkinson (UK/USA), *Mining Culture in Technicolour*, (details both images same piece) *The Land That They Live on is Like Their Mother*, Slip cast earthenware, low fire decals and gold lustre, 1998, collection University College of Wales, Aberystwyth. Photo A. Vincentelli.

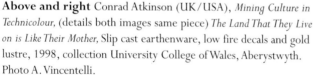

An artist with strong political and ideological principles, Atkinson is an habitual 'visitor' to different materials and disciplines, using whichever medium is appropriate to the subject matter of his work. Trained as a painter he has variously worked with newspapers (designs for posters based on the front pages of the Wall Street Journal, The Financial Times *and* The Guardian, *the last of which subsequently actually produced it as its front page), steel fabrications, rubber, carpets, red glittery shoes and painting too. As the Official Artist to the Organisation to Ban Land Mines in the USA, Atkinson began to produce ceramic land-mines in 1997. 'If land mines had been used in the (US) Civil War at the current rate of clean up, they'd still be there, so you wouldn't be able to let your children walk across the grass today . . . basically at the current rate of removal it's going to take another thousand years to eliminate all the land-mines scattered throughout the world, even if they stop laying them right away.' Basing the form on a land mine produced in Europe, Atkinson has placed a variety of*

images on their surfaces, from Willow patterns to images of Princess Diana. These have then been variously placed in exhibitions and museums. In Carlisle the bombs were exhibited amongst the collection of European porcelain. Our industrialised society producing bombs with the same care as it produces porcelain, and sold in the same way to whoever will buy them with no thought for their consequences.

In Atlanta: 'I thought, okay, I love Gone With the Wind, so I'll use that imagery in some way. Then I was really surprised at my reaction to Diana, the Princess of Wales' death. I thought, I can't touch this, but then I thought no, why shouldn't I touch this? I wanted to make an image that was very powerful, popular, and pervasive, one that outmanoeuvred advertising and its images. I wanted to find a popular image and make a work of art that was popular as well as a container for several different meanings. Diana's image, on the one hand, can be seen as maudlin or it can be seen as exploitative. On the other hand, it can be seen as a souvenir, as kitsch. You've got all these issues to negotiate. So the land mines eventually ended up painted with the Ashley Wilkes board from Gone With the Wind, only changed to Diana's name and placed with ceramic mines containing the image of Diana walking through land mines.' (Conrad Atkinson quoted in 'From the Political to the Popular', Sculpture, September 1998.)

CHAPTER 5

More Visitors, the Emergence of Studio Pottery

Studio ceramics as a genre has evolved relatively recently, and its growth has differed according to location. It is tempting to make generalisations about its growth in whole countries, but in doing so, it should be remembered that the dominant and accepted history is not always inclusive enough of minority practice, nor does it always reflect regional differences. There are always vested interests promoting particular views, philosophies or angles, and accounts (including this one) should always be treated with some degree of scepticism.

The acceptance by the French that its painters and sculptors will make forays into areas of the 'applied arts', seems well established, and with the precedence of the first two thirds of the 20th century, it is hardly surprising. However, in the Anglo-American art world, until recently, this acceptance has been seldom found, tolerated or even acknowledged; instead narrower areas of practice, study and discipline seem to have evolved.

When the study of ceramics and the identification of the 'artist potter' evolved in the second half of the 20th century in Britain, it appears to have come from two sources: the philosophies and writing of Bernard Leach, and the design movement linked to industry. The guiding philosophies behind both have been concerned with lifestyle, form, production and design. They have run almost parallel; occasionally raising a metaphorical head above the wall that divides their narrow agendas to lob cursory jibes or obscure references at each other, they have ostensibly cre-

ated two separate areas of study. Like the writing, documentation and exhibitions of the 'fine arts', the craft pottery movement in particular has a serious blind spot when it comes to ceramics involving the graphic development of surface; the whole area is regarded as being completely irrelevant, unless the decoration in question is entirely subservient to form and function. Its role although more elevated in industrial, design-based study, is still to do with the design of objects and their decoration.

That this came about is probably a result of the innate conservatism of the British, but it might not have been like this.

Leach, Studio Pottery, Staite Murray, Haile and Washington

Whilst the French and Italians were using clay as another art material, Bernard Leach arrived in England accompanied by apprentice Shoji Hamada and set up a pottery in St Ives on the Cornish coast. His philosophy was that the potter should be solely responsible for the whole clay process from digging and mixing raw materials to throwing, glazing and decoration. He believed that pots should be made for everyday use, and should be informed by classic, but selected, periods in ceramic history. He was inspirational in his teachings, and eventually, his book *The Potter's Book* (published in 1940), an articulate but fundamentally flawed treatise on ceramics, was simply the only one available for a long time.

There was an alternative voice at an early stage, in the figure of William Staite Murray, who regarded the pot as an object of contemplation. Both Staite Murray and Leach associated with painters and sculptors of major international importance 'amongst whom were Ben Nicholson, Barbara Hepworth, Christopher Wood, Naum Gabo (the Russian Constructivist sculptor) and his brother Antoine Pevsner. Their influence on each other in their rapidly developing styles and the effects of contact with Brancusi, Mondrian and Georges Braque in Europe is quite clear, but Bernard Leach remained statistically the outsider, with no cross-fertilisation of ideas, his inspiration and thoughts focused predominantly on Japan and the East' [41].

Staite Murray was more open, interested and accommodating. He became Professor of Ceramics at the Royal College of Art in London. 'Murray at the RCA was trying to prove that there was no difference between the students in the Painting School and those in the Pottery School . . . he gave us belief in our validity as ceramic artists' (Robert Washington 1984). Two of his pupils in particular, Sam Haile and Robert Washington, are of interest for they indicated a route where painting and ceramics began to come together as they were doing in France, but sadly their moves were to come to premature ends.

Sam Haile was primarily a painter: 'as a member of the British Surrealist Group, there is little doubt that Haile thought himself to be first and foremost a painter; pottery being a secondary concern' [42]. However, his time at the Royal College was far from easy. Interested in Picasso, Matisse, Klee and Moore, his Surrealist paintings were not favoured, and when informed that if he 'continued to paint like a barbarian' no diploma would be given, he transferred to the pottery department. As others in similar circumstances have also since found, the pottery department given the right circumstances (usually the right teacher) can be a liberating place for a painter. Accounts of Staite Murray's role as teacher cast him as an unconventional type: it seems he taught little technique, and offered little constructive criticism. He himself is supposed to have said: 'I don't teach, I create an atmosphere.'

This approach suited both Haile and Washington (another painter) and their ceramics of this period, although generally muted brown stonewares, were a radical departure from the conventional. Their forms appear to have been influenced by Staite Murray (although Washington claimed

[41] John Maltby in *Ceramic Review* 12, 1990
[42] Victor Margrie in *Sam Haile, Potter and Painter*, Bellew 1993

Left R. J. Washington (UK), Female and male decoration in red iron on vase form, 57.5 cm (22.5") 1981. Photo by R. J. Washington. From the Core collection of the estate of R. J. Washington.

Above Sam Haile (UK), plate, 1941. Jigger jollied with direct silkscreen print. Photo Kate Mount, collection of Marianne Haile.

never to have seen a pot of his until after the Second World war), but the surfaces were used as vehicles for Surrealistic and Cubist paintings. Haile is reported to have spent hours in the British Museum studying not only the Tang and Sung (which had so inspired Leach), but also the Minoan, Cycladic, English Mediaeval and other ceramics which presumably also included Italian maiolica. Both showed their work and received critical attention; writing of Haile, *New Statesman* said, 'the most interesting pottery now being made in this country. Mr Haile finds inspiration for his ornament not in China but in primitive art, and in archaic Greek work. The results are personal, felicitous and often poetical in suggestion'[43].

The Second World War saw Haile and his wife Marianne in the USA, where Garth Clark describes his impact as being 'considerable'. Teaching at Alfred University he found the Americans much less obsessed with form and utility. His 'glazes were informal creations of a small number of of materials. He replaced perfection with the expressive power of his pots'. His palette was limited, but his pots were expressive not only because of his methodology of throwing, but also because of the attention and importance he placed on their surfaces. During his time there he experimented with direct screenprinting on jigger jollied forms. This is at a time before screenprinting was used commercially on ceramics, and he was possibly the first artist to explore something of its potential.

Haile returned to England in 1944, and died in a motor accident four years later. Washington demobbed, entered the teaching profession and followed a career in education, only returning to serious ceramic production on his retirement in 1974. By then the ceramics world was a different place, but even then his painterly sensibilities were still out of sync with the contemporary scene: 'I am in a limbo . . . rejected as a potter and unclassifiable as a painter'[44] . 'I am enjoying my ceramic sculpture, which seems easier for people to accept than painting – bloody stupid – I regard this as a final absurdity. If ceramics can be sculpture and thus Fine Art why cannot it be Fine Art painting?'.[45]

Above R. J. Washington (UK), *Earth Air Fire and Water, Platter type II,* Stoneware, multi-fired, painted with engobes, 56 cm (22") dia., 1987. Photo R. J. Washington. From the Core collection of the estate of R. J. Washington.

[43] quoted in *Sam Haile, Potter and Painter*, Bellew 1993
[44] quoted in 'Body and Soul', *Ceramic Review*, 174
[45] R. J. Washington, in a letter to Peter Dormer 14/6/94

He was quite clear in his belief that ceramics was a valid medium for a painter, and without necessarily the baggage of painting on forms: 'I have prepared gesso grounds — made and ground my colours-primed panels with glue of the old hoof variety — undercoated, glossed — mixed varnishes — made boiled oil and can fairly claim to know the qualities and potentiality of most painting media. Therefore when I say to you that the painted form of expression through the qualities of silica and its fluxes in the fire give me a satisfaction and an end product in no way similar to any other, you surely have to accept its validity . . . I claim to be no different from any other painter, i.e. a watercolourist does not work happily in egg temper, any more

Below R. J. Washington (UK), *Lunar Eclipse*, painted engobes on ceramic fibre panel, 71 cm x 61 cm (28" x 24") 1990/1992. Photo R. J. Washington. From the Core collection of the estate of R. J. Washington.

Towards the end of his life Washington experimented with the creation of large ceramic canvases, incorporating ceramic fibre in the clay body (like paperclay) to enable him to make large flat tiles for paintings. 'The plastic clay provides the potter with all his options of impressing, scratching, taking away and applying processes. The engobes enable the painter to experience his pleasures in thin washes, heavy impasto, knifing, scumbling etc. He also has a bonus because the three-dimensionally treated clay surface is so much more exciting to paint upon than a plain primed canvas and the facets add colour to colours' (R. J. Washington, 1984).

than an oil painter would be happy in fresco and its rigid limitations; thus I state, without having to be conscious of prejudice, convention or kitsch, that I am a Painter working in the painting medium of his choice and having a security based upon his early training'[46].

The result of the loss of these figures who were involving serious painterly concerns with the ceramic surface

Below Maggie Angus Berkowitz (UK), *Mela in an Apple Tree.* Painting in glaze on white earthenware tiles.

meant that in postwar Britain, the stage was clear for the domination of the utilitarian and later, with the influence of Hans Coper and Lucie Rie, form-based ceramics. In both these schools, painted surface was either minimal, irrelevant or viewed with downright hostility.

Swimming against the tide

With this background those who approached ceramics from other perspectives were actively discouraged, and found it hard to rise to the surface. However, over the years there were some with alternative sensibilities who survived and carved out a niche for their work in this craft pottery world, adapting their working methods and philosophies to the predominant ideologies. The following are ceramists of longstanding in Britain, who have swum against the current at times, but who have survived and still operate within the world of studio pottery, enriching the surface with strong painting and drawing.

Maggie Berkowitz is predominantly a tile painter. She recalls making pictures with glass beads as a child ('Looking back they were my first glazed pictures'). She went on to college during the Second World War to train as an illustrator ('art to earn a living') and remembers the restrictions on materials that informed what could be studied. There were also very few magazines or sources of information about pictures, but there were pictures of images on pots and later working on production pottery she was occasionally allowed to make and paint tiles. She vividly remembers reading Cipriano Piccolpasso's book *Three Books of the Potter's Art* and with the help of an Italian Government grant, was able to study maiolica in Faenza, Italy. She was aware of Italian fine artists working with ceramics in Milan, but later working in the USA, she found that the Leach tradition had instilled a deep hostility both to earthenware and painting on clay. Over the years since her return to England, she has developed a unique palette of glazes, and painting and drawing processes. Operating on the edge of the craft pottery world she has worked mainly to commission for many years.

Eric Mellon: The Leach emphasis of truth to raw materials, and the necessity of making glazes is seen in Eric Mellon's life long affair with ash glazes, but Mellon is far from the the archetypal glaze pourer and dipper. His quest has been for a clear transparent glassy layer through which

[46] R. J. Washington, in a letter to Peter Dormer 14/6/94

his paintings and drawings in metal oxides can shine through with clarity. 'The beautiful colours I wanted came at higher temperatures and as colouring oxides are mostly fluxes the problems seemed endless.' In 1958 he became a member of the Craft Potters Association, and in the same year began his long quest for ash glaze quality. 'Many ashes were tested including pine, willow, elm, pear, blackcurrant, cypress, beech, horse chestnut and privet . . . this led to an understanding that some tree ashes are high in calcium oxide, whereas bush ashes are high in silica oxide'[47].

[47] Eric Mellon in *Ceramic Review* 114, 1988

Above Eric Mellon (UK), *Sleeping Maiden*, painting, porcelain bowl, 9.5cm (3.75") dia., horse chestnut ash glaze. Photo Chris Hodow.
'Iron oxide fires to the colour of a conker with yellow flashing. Difficult to use on stoneware bodies and kiln losses are inevitable if decorated. Being a tree ash it is high in calcium.'

This now almost encyclopaedic knowledge has enabled him to use colouring oxides at temperatures in excess of 1300°C without undue distortion, or bleeding of the drawing on the clay body. His paintings on and in pots are carefully constructed with reference to rules of composition. Mellon writes: 'The study of composition seems much neglected by potters and apart from vertical and horizontal

marks and diagonal marks balancing each other, ceramic decoration remains for the most part limited. Books and demonstrations generally only deal with methods of decoration and no more. For our aesthetic needs the first priority is a vertical line or form (totem poles and columns). This is followed by a horizontal line. Followed by diagonal lines and a circular movement. Variety is essential and for this visual balance, the Greek golden mean or section or other geometric division to be held in the 'mind' to produce subtle visual satisfaction. The development in painting

Above Eric Mellon (UK), *Persephone With a Musician and Ascalaphus (Owl) and a Maiden*, painting; hymod, Molochite and china clay bowl, 28 cm (11") dia., cherry ash glaze. Photo Chris Hodow.

Mellon's subject matters have varied over the years; he has covered politics including the US war in Vietnam, the use of defoliant 245T, Biafra and Northern Ireland, but he is known especially for his drawings and paintings of human figure, and spends much time life drawing.

Right John Maltby (UK), *Harbour with Boat*, tankard form, stoneware, 30 cm x 30 cm (12" x 12").

follows through vertical and horizontal stabilities of the 15th century; diagonal and cartwheel constructions in the 16th century; figure of eight compositions. The examples of Rembrandt's composition drawings and use of space a perpetual source of learning. A line will only remain so until it completes and joins; then it has become a shape, a visual area. These three things are all that an artist can use apart from tone and colour. Picasso's ceramic follows exactly on the use of these simple rules as do the paintings of Modigliani – lines, shapes and areas' [47]. He clearly identifies his work as being in the 'tradition of visual art', and once proclaimed that ceramics to be the 'greatest art form'. 'Drawing into clay is firing thoughts into clay that can remain as no other material can.'

[48] Eric Mellon in Ceramic Review 114, 1988

John Maltby is another who has striven to use painting and imagery within his work over many years. Struggling to reconcile Leach's vision of the East bizarrely transposed to become identified as quintessentially English studio pottery, he writes: 'I have tried in my own way to find a common ground on which I might feel more easily relaxed than upon this Anglo-Oriental source.' Maltby has identified with the 'Englishness of English Art', and in his works seek to convey his love of the English rural landscape: churches, sea, rocks, birds and flowers. However, he is not averse to some oriental inspiration, referring with affection and admiration to the pots of the Japanese Ogata Kenzan in which the ceramic object is used as a 'conscious vehicle for personal and intimate expression'. His ceramics are idiosyncratic, he relishes accident and imperfection, the childlike and the simple. His forms, sometimes with nods to function, lean slightly, their surfaces richly but simply and abstractedly painted.

Robin Welch helped in the Leach pottery in the mid-1950s before enrolling in the Central School of Arts and Crafts in London in 1958. Gordon Baldwin, one of his tutors, taught that there were no rules, that within your own aims and integrity you could do anything. This approach was to shake up some of the preconceptions which had developed about pottery, and when he then travelled to Australia, the grounds for his later work were set. Deeply affected by the antipodean landscape, he met Australian painters Tom Gleghorn, Emmanuel Raft and others. Welch has continued to travel to the other side of the world as often as he can, observing that the Australian landscape has dramatic colour and a primal, 'ceramic feel'. He has consistently painted and drawn throughout his career, and ceramic work has been only a (albeit significant) part of his total production. Having started as a potter it has been natural for Welch to use ceramic materials for painting and drawing. He uses a white matt glaze originally produced at the Central as his 'primer' for the surface, then proceeds to paint with glaze and oxide and prepared

Left Robin Welch (UK), one of a series of large paintings with pots. Painting and pot in same colour way. Series included black, white, red, blue, yellow, green, orange. Paintings on canvas using acrylics and oils. Pots arranged in front of hung paintings on painted stands. Pot 85 cm (33.5") ht, thrown and hand-built with coils and slabs, porcelain slip with red underglaze colours, reduction fired to 1300°C. Low temperature earthenware red glaze added and fired to 1080°C. 1992. Collection Mr & Mrs Oliver Knowland.

Above Robin Welch (UK), cylindrical vase, 15 cm x 12 cm (6" x 4.75") dia., 1997, thrown and turned crank mixture with porcelain slip patches, lustre glaze, manganese dioxide and china clay, blue and black velvet underglazes. 1280°C reduction firing. Collection Alastair James.

underglaze colours. He then fires, observes, and contemplates the result before maybe reapplying a colour or glaze and refiring until the surface is resolved.

He believes that it is much easier today to use ceramics as a painterly medium because a whole range of colours and materials are out there to buy and use. In the early days of studio ceramics, to paint you also needed a considerable knowledge of ceramic chemistry (and most of the chemistry was directed at glazes, and not the painterly use of them), and a determination and vision to work in a way not necessarily in tune with the prevailing mood of the day.

John Pollex had carved out a niche in the world of studio pottery, over the years establishing himself as a respected maker of traditional slipware, before his work took a dramatic turn. He came into contact with the work of contemporary American ceramists including Don Reitz whilst on lecture tours in USA and New Zealand, and their impact was substantial. The bold use of colour was appealing compared to the muted tones of celadons, tenmokus and honey glazes and back in Britain, he became less and less happy with his production: 'In 1981 my daughter Kate was born and I found myself spending less time in the workshop. As she grew and we played together I realised that she was enjoying herself more than I was. It was then, in 1984, I decided to change everything'[49].

Referring to the work of painters such as Howard Hodgkin, Robert Natkin, Patrick Heron and Ben Nicholson, Pollex used his knowledge and understanding of the application of slips to develop a completely different style of working. Dispensing with slip trailers in favour of paintbrushes and sponges, intensely coloured earthenware slips were applied in a free, painterly and abstract manner. The change seems to have been clean and dramatic and appears to owe nothing to the slipware of before. However, Pollex himself indicates that although the methodology was completely different, his mind set and whole approach to working took some time to evolve. He first produced 'batches' of work, almost repetition pieces, until gradually and eventually his confidence

[49] John Pollex, in *Ceramic Review* 132, 1991

Right John Pollex (UK), *Tall Jug*, 27 cm (10.5") ht. Buff earthenware with painted and sponged slips.

Right John Pollex (UK), *Square Dish,* 29 cm x 29 cm (11.5" x 11.5"). Buff earthenware with painted and sponged slips.

and working methods grew so that each piece became an individual composition. Unlike most painting practice, Pollex uses a black ground onto which intensely coloured slips are painted and sponged. Because of the opacity of coloured slip, the bright colours are not adversely affected by the black ground, and the spaces between painted areas appear as black outlines. Although Pollex's work has evolved from functional domestic ware, 'in the more recent work the idea of function is now becoming secondary to the process of making and painting. Altered forms often suggest the marks and shapes that will eventually appear. I now see my work in the area of three-dimensional painting whereby clay substitutes canvas. The ceramic discs I make serve no other function than to be looked at' [50].

The philosophies and working practices of these five were in many ways peripheral to the traditional studio potter, and that they have established reputations in what could be seen as a hostile environment, says much about the tolerance and

camaraderie of studio potters. It also says much about the strength of their personalities and work that they have survived and thrived as members of the Craft Potters Association. This organisation of studio potters is basically an artist run co-operative, and its achievements are impressive, running a gallery and shop just off Oxford Street in London, and starting the much respected magazine *Ceramic Review.* However, the perception that the CPA represents the 'best of British ceramics', and their historical role in acting as a selective 'taste police' has not been universally popular. There are major figures in British ceramics who have had no association with the organisation, establishing themselves either as high profile applied or fine artists, exhibiting and selling exclusively through the appropriate galleries.

Two of these important figures are Alison Britton and Elizabeth Fritsch. They both make pots, and although their work is very different they are both involved and absorbed with the painterly or graphic. Both studied at the Royal College in London, and both were influenced by their tutor Hans Coper. For Coper and his close associate Lucie Rie the

[50] John Pollex, in *Ceramic Review* 132, 1991

pot was an art object, not necessarily a utilitarian container implying possible use. This concept of the ceramic form was less dogmatic, and inherently freer than that of the Leach tradition, and it produced a new breed of 'makers' who explored ceramics in a modern, sculptural manner. For both Fritsch and Britton, painterly sensibilities inform and deeply affect the way they approach the making and composition of these new three dimensional works.

Elizabeth Fritsch initially trained as a musician, and she has made no secret of the fact that she sees close parallels between her ceramics and musical structures. In her 'Notes on new work 1992' she writes: 'The three main channels of expression in the work are colour, form and rhythm, and the primary preoccupation is with the way these three aspects can be made to activate and emphasise each other.' Fritsch's interests besides jazz and encyclopaedic reading,

Above Alison Britton (UK), *Yellow Jug with Blue Painting*, 40 cm x 38 cm x 24 cm (16" x 15" x 9.5"), 1995. Photograph David Cripps.

'I'd be loathe to stop painting. I see it as one of the jobs that pottery can do and nothing else can do — that mixture of having a concern for the painted surface and having a concern for form. That is what is special about ceramics' (Alison Britton 1989).

'The largely unwritten history of studio ceramics has been dominated by an unimaginative reading of Bernard Leach's creative philosophy. By the late sixties many of Leach's admirers came to believe that he was primarily committed to making functional ware and that this was the proper work of the potter. Since then it has become usual to say that the work of Alison Britton and her contemporaries belongs to a much older tradition — of non functional ceramics that have the status of treasure — (to use Philip Rawson's phrase) and which tend to reflect the fine art of a period. Thus fifteenth century maiolica, eighteenth century Meissen and Sèvres and nineteenth century art pottery are all invoked to give context to the work of Alison Britton' (Tanya Harrod in Alison Britton, Ceramics in Studio, Bellew/Aberystwyth Arts Centre 1990).

Left Elizabeth Fritsch (UK), *Over the Edge, Blown Away* vases, 56 cm (22"). Photo Sarah Morris.

'The dialogue in colour is between the strong, vivid, unbroken colours (these are sometimes stains designed for industrial use) combined with the more 'earthy', shaded or speckled aspects of colour (provided by metal oxides, etc., and the use of colour, in layers of impasto, etc.)' (Elizabeth Fritsch, from Elizabeth Fritsch, Vessels from Another World, Metaphysical Pots in Painted Stoneware, Bellew/Northern Centre for Contemporary Art, 1993).

include the paintings of Piero della Francesca, Surrealism, the Russian Suprematist Malevich, and the Argentinean writer Jorge Luis Borges. Elements of this eclectic mix can be discerned in her enigmatic pots which seem to occupy a space between two and three dimensions. Identified once as 'vessels from another world' Fritsch builds by hand, her forms built spontaneously using experience and instinct. Similarly the painting on the surface is conceived to relate to and answer the shape. 'The painting adds another layer, or sometimes a series of layers. It often seems to exist in an illusory space which lies within the volume of the vessel; that is it actually penetrates the surface. However the surface it penetrates is frequently an illusion too, not something which corresponds with the actual form. The rhythm of her applied shapes is such that it makes space twist and bend. The deception is often deliberately revealed by allowing the developing patterns to collide in an apparently random fashion'[51].

Alison Britton has also been the constructor of abstracted forms with a painterly surface. Initially setting aside the sculptural aspirations of some of her contemporaries, she embarked on a 'playful yet searching look at everyday forms'. Her early work was very illustrative, yet interpreted Leach's carefully developed language of pottery form, taking the 'generous handle', 'beak' or 'lip' and the pots 'belly' to 'shoulder' with rather less reverence, and in a completely different context than the originator. Over a period of time she has developed a much more abstracted and painterly approach to the surface; she has evolved an approach to pot making that removes the functional, but that explores the volumes and surfaces of 'the vessel', moving the subject into the sculptural and painted sphere.

These individuals working in Britain have been key players in this field, and show that the dominance of the Leach aesthetic has not been an entirely negative one. Several have adapted ways of working within a context that was largely created by the Leach philosophies. In doing this, their drives to work painterly and graphically in a medium associated with pottery form and utility have produced work that has broken new grounds in studio ceramics, and created pieces that literally straddle the rigidly defined areas of visual arts practice.

[51] Edward Lucie-Smith in *Elizabeth Fritsch, Vessels from Another World, Metaphysical Pots in Painted Stoneware,* Bellew/Northern Centre for Contemporary Art, 1993

Above John Maltby (UK), *East Anglian Church (Cold)*, stoneware,
25 cm x 25 cm (10" x 10").

*'I have been told that most of my ceramics lean slightly, either in form or in
pattern, or both. This is not a conscious intention, but perhaps part of that
subliminal consciousness which I have tried to describe and which pervades our
natures. (I remember as a small boy leaning into the fierce winds of the east
coast where I was born.) The patterns, often motifs of harbours, boats and nets
come from this background and from the coastal villages of the southwest
peninsula in which I live: images of Wells Cathedral, Suffolk churches or
English gardens frequently appear, but it is the resolution of form and pattern
in equal and complementary balance that is the recurring challenge'*
(John Maltby in Ceramic Review *122, 1990).*

CHAPTER 6

North America, Vessels and Surface

North American studio ceramics

Garth Clark, ceramics gallery owner and historian[52] has observed that 'an archaeologist some two thousand years from now digging through the shard piles of the early 1950s might well deduce that at this moment Japan and China had banished all their failed potters to the United States', so widespread was Leach's influence in North America. However, unlike Britain where the monoculture of domestic pottery took deep root and smothered alternatives, the American experience was of swift diversification as other personalities, movements, and cultural differences informed the growth of studio ceramics producing a more eclectic mix of studio practice.

The lack of a tight tie to centuries of tradition and conservatism (which hung so heavy around the neck of the British) allowed ceramists in North America to take from a variety of sources, from Pop Art, Abstract Expressionism, and from Leach. The results were the Funk movement originated by Robert Arneson at Davis, the Super Object characterised by leader Richard Shaw's surreal porcelain assemblages, and Peter Volkous.

Volkous, a one-time producer of domestic pottery, taught at the Otis School in Los Angeles in the 1950s. He was indelibly affected by the ceramics of Picasso, the Jomon, Shigaraki and Bizen pottery of Japan, and most significantly by the painters of the Abstract Expressionist movement. 'The pots produced at Otis were an attack on the stultifying mores of Western pottery. The forms were aggressively asymmetrical. The surfaces were competitive with the form, not politely subservient as was the tradition.' [53]

In contrast, based at University of California at Davis, Bob Arneson's big, bold work introduced references to commercial mass production in studio ceramics. It was sculptural, irreverent, vulgar, confrontational and political. The ceramics of Super Realism by Richard Shaw on the other hand were cool, trompe l'oeil. He used the facility of ceramics, both clay and graphic surface, to perfectly mimic other objects, to create surreal assemblages of cigarette boxes, playing cards, books and other everyday objects.

From this mix came Howard Kottler, who helped to redefine American ceramic art; referencing the super object, Duchamp, industrially-produced pottery, kitsch, and camp. His witty and ironic ceramic work used pots, sculpture and plates, and included the use of decals to create trompe l'oeil. Later, by cutting and collaging commercial decals he was able to combine surrealist methods of image disruption with social satire (See *Howard Kottler Face to Face*, Patricia Failing, University of Washington Press 1995).

Kottler's work would have been more at home within the fine art arena than the craft one in which it sometimes found itself, and there have been running battles

[52] & [53] Garth Clarke in 'American Ceramics since 1950', *American Ceramics, The collection of the Everson Museum of Art*, Rizzoli International Publications Inc., 1989

Gainsborough Blue Boy, fish paste lid, FR Pratt Ware c. 1860. Polychrome underglaze print. Photo courtesy of Paul Mason. Victorian pot lids for a short period were produced using four or five colour engravings. Favourite subjects included reproductions of famous paintings.

Above Howard Kottler (USA), *Split Personality,* decal collage on porcelain plate c. 1968, 27 cm (10.5") dia. Photo Eduardo Caulderon, courtesy Garth Clark Gallery, New York.

over the years with some (hopelessly unrealistically) attempting to re-locate the whole of ceramics into the fine art arena. Some denounce the attempts to identify works with fine art movements or styles as an unnecessary prostitution of the ceramic genre. The argument goes that ceramics has a sound philosophical base, with enough tradition and innovative practice, and does not need to imitate or shadow the fine arts, but just be itself.

Whatever the merits of the debate, the result is that many contemporary ceramists accept that their work, and its rich traditions, fit well in the current broad visual arts market and economy. In the USA the work of certain ceramists are perceived as being of the same value (philosophically and economically) as the work of fine artists working in other disciplines or areas.

Clark has identified American contemporary ceramics as operating in two distinct worlds: ceramic sculpture and the vessel. 'The world of the vessel has grown into an artistically credible genre of its own.' Within that genre (which presumably includes the glazed reductions of thrown forms and wood-fired salt glazed vessels, of little interest here) are a significant group whose vessel forms include a particularly graphic development of the surface. Within this (sub) group there are deep philosophical differences and debates, but they are held together, at least superficially, by an interest in the embellishment of the surface.

Classic forms

This vessel world is not just an American manifestation, there are ceramists from Canada, Europe and Australia whose work fits the description too. It is from Canada that the most intellectual, studied exploration and use of form, volume and surface has come in the works of Leopold Foulem, Richard Milette, and Paul Mathieu. The intellectual reasoning behind their works may not be immediately apparent to the casual viewer, but the very nature of the work, relying on essentially classical and universal pottery forms, makes it immediately widely accessible.

In addition to the initial familiarity of forms (which are not always so conventional on closer examination), a key to the viewers involvement in the works is the graphic use of the surface. The use of printed or painted imagery involves another thread of communication which continues to draw in the unaware to unravel more information about the subject of the work . . . for these are not just decorative pots, they are loaded with meaning and intent.

For readers of this book, and the vast majority of people who see this work, Mathieu asserts that the experience of

Above Leopold Foulem (Canada), *Famille Verte 'with Blue Boy in Closet'*.
Cylindrical covered jar 37 cm x 27 cm x 14 cm (14.5" x 10.75" x 5 ½")
1994–1996. Photo R. Bergeron. Both Kottler and Foulem say: 'We are not
only using the same Victorian icon, but also dealing with the identical
issue of being in the closet, or having a split personality . . . Howard
Kottler was also gay,' Léopold Foulem.

his work is not a full one, for that to be so the viewer must also hold, touch and handle his objects. In not doing so, there is a tangible loss of experience and understanding.

It is of course true, but it is also undeniably true of sculpture and painting too. The experience of actually 'being' with a work of art, of physically seeing for the first time is universally a memorable event. No colour print or reproduction however fine can substitute for the real thing. However, through the advent of quality colour printing we all benefit from access to images and sights that just a few years ago were only in the realm of the wealthy and fortunate few. The work of these ceramists, and all those who use paint, print and graphics on the surface, or as part of their forms, are well suited to the new high definition,

Above Paul Mathieu (Canada), *The Arrows of Time (for SWH),* 1989. Seven pieces of painted porcelain. 46 cm x 46 cm x 30 cm (18" x 18" x 12").

Above Paul Mathieu (Canada), *The Arrows of Time (for SWH)*, 1989, disassembled. Seven pieces of painted porcelain. 46 cm x 46 cm x 30 cm (18" x 18" x 12").

'Pottery accumulates time and preserves it' (Paul Mathieu). This piece (or pieces) was conceived after reading physicist Stephen Hawkins on time; Hawkins identifies three different aspects or arrows of time, and Mathieu uses the composition to illustrate the definitions. The first arrow of time is the psychological aspect, the human understanding of past, present and future time. This is found in the images of the passing of time, the pouring, and later drinking. The Second is the Entropic arrow of time, ever more complex and irreversible shown by the disassemblage of the elements of the composition, the Third the Cosmological extension shown by the image of the small teapot growing to fill the larger space.

As well as the illustrative and physical characteristics of the piece combining together to create the work, there is the added trompe l'oeil quality of his work, 'Void and mass are camouflaged, veiled by drawn three-dimensional images on two-dimensional surfaces, or volumes and perspective flattened with painted two-dimensional imagery. The problems of representation of realistic two- and three-dimensional drawing and foreshortening on flat and curved surfaces have always been of primary concern for vase painters, not only Roman trompe l'oeil muralists and Renaissance easel painters, as has been reiterated by Western art historians. Mathieu uses plates as canvas is used as support and he uses cups and teapots to refer to three-dimensional form. Form and volume are shown as inseparable in ceramics. The decoration carried through the levels or layers of dishes unifies the narrative while alluding to collage in its references to superimposition' (Gloria Lessing in 'Getting to the Heart of the Matter', in Ceramics Art and Perception 12, 1993).

Left Leopold Foulem, (Canada), *I love my Daddy,* ceramic and found objects, 37.5 cm x 12 cm x 12 cm (15" x 4.75" x 4.75"), 1994–1996, from Des Mots et des Images, Montréal 1997. Collection Musée du Québec. Photograph R. Bergeron.

Foulem's ceramic objects are unusable; constructed around secondhand silver-plate and found objects, made from earthenware with simple glazes adorned with mass produced decals. They imitate the precious ceramics of past times, but they are not. Foulem uses symbols that have already been cornered by the kitsch market, to which he adds double entendres through implication. Some of the images also have specific meaning in gay society. I Love my Daddy *features the regulation image of Christ with the crown of thorns and although it seems an innocent enough reference to Christian and Catholic imagery, on a form reminiscent of a reliquary, it is in fact an oblique reference to sadomasochism which is usually not only perceived in our society as a perverse sexual practice, but is often equated with homosexual sex.*

Leopold Foulem has said of his work: 'My work is never creative. Creative means that I put my stamp on it and that is not important. Ideas are the essence. The forms are my forms but they are not really my forms because I deal in stereotypes. I use a stereotype so that everyone will understand. I am not trying to expand the category as far as form is concerned, I am trying to force people to focus on the object or icon. This makes a valid rather than new signifier.'

'My work does not have to do with nostalgia, but with intimacy and domesticity. Also my work does not have anything to do with contemplation. It has to do with discourse – the relationship with the object, the object's relationship to culture and culture's relationship to you the viewer. My work is not as simple as it looks. It is not as easy as it looks, although it is not contrived. My work has nothing to do with with self-expression. It has to do with expression. Also there are aspects of ceramic history, history of form, history of taste that are relevant. My work is not about taste, it is about the history of taste' (Léopold Foulem, in 'Abstraction and Contradiction, the Ceramics of Leopold Foulem', an Interview by Wendy Walgate, Ceramics Art and Perception *24, 1996).*

Right Richard Milette, (Canada), *Skyphos with blue and white lid,* from *Jarring Dissonance, Vessel texts: Songs sans Tales.* Ceramic, 29.5 cm x 32.5 cm x 22.5 cm (11.5" x 12.75" x 9"). Photo courtesy of Nancy Margolis Gallery, New York.

'By abstracting the most fetishistic part of classical Greek vases, and treating the framed area where myths (tales) are painted as a palimpset, the artist takes over both the art of painting and the craft of pottery. The vessel becomes a whole where all parts are components of equal importance. The ceramic object must now be re-evaluated for its own merit. In the recontextualization process the neo-Greek vase has now become the image of itself' (Leopold Foulem on Jarring Dissonance).

graphic reproductions in glossy magazines and books. Seductiveness and meaning created by images and marks are more easily and universally communicated and appreciated than the runs and drips of salt or wood ash glazes. Even on unconventional forms created by the new ceramics of the 20th century the use of line, colour and graphic image act to draw the viewer in to an involvement in a complex piece.

Foulem, Mathieu, and Milette all believe that the ceramic form in dealing with volume, and being created by volume, provides for the combination of both painting and sculpture together, that it needs not aspire to either, but uniquely provides both and more. Each has burrowed into slightly different, but related aspects of ceramic history, philosophies and practice, but with the sensibilities and ideas of artists operating at the very end of the 20th century.

Another Canadian, Greg Payce also references ceramic history in his use of imagery, pattern, banding and form, but his is a formal rather than social commentary, employing concept in his play of positive and negative space. Inspired by Sèvres vase garnitures and rows of Italian Renaissance albarellos, his recent works use the negative spaces between pottery forms as windows and/or images.

Much less formal, but using the language of form as the vehicle for decorative subversion, Grayson Perry's ceramics caused consternation and controversy in studio pottery when first shown in the UK. The dislike was not one way: 'One of the main inspirations when I started using clay was how much I loathed all contemporary ceramics . . .' [54]. Sometimes referred to as 'crude', his rugged, overtly coiled, hand-built forms are in fact covered in intense graphic detail and decoration created by a rich combination of techniques from sgraffito, slip layering and carving, painting, sprigging and the frequent use of printed decals. Any crudity is inferred by the sexual nature of some of his subjects, and the scratching in or stamping of everyday words used by a large proportion of the population, some more often seen on toilet walls than on pottery. His overtly sexual and autobiographical pieces often refer to his other persona, Claire, but his subject matters are wide and varied, and include the fine art world.

[54] Grayson Perry in 'Fear and Loathing', *AN*, July 1994

Above left Greg Payce, (Canada), *Trio*. Red earthenware, terra sigilatta, slips, resist and glazes. 48 cm x 18 cm x 27 cm (19" x 7" x 10.5"), 1997.

'The negative spaces between four chalices forms a trio of cellos. The painting on the tile behind the chalices is a musical score over passionflower vines.'

Left Greg Payce, (Canada), *Quartet Vase*, 1997. Red earthenware, terra sigilatta, slips, resist and glazes, 42 cm (16.5") ht. This vase has a two-dimensional rendering of *Trio* on its neck.

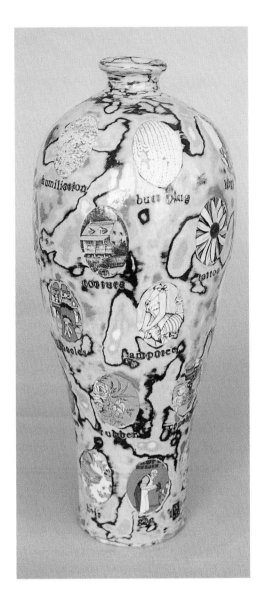

Above Grayson Perry (UK), *Transference*.
Earthenware, with decals. 51 cm (20") ht. 1996.
Collection of Anthony D'Offay.

*Obliquely referring to fetishes and the transference of
emotions to objects (also a play on the use of transfers
(decals) on the ceramic surface). 'I have always played up
the fact that pottery isn't taken seriously in fine art. It
lends my work a kitsch irony and another layer of
meaning' (Grayson Perry in 'Fear and Loathing', AN,
July 1994).*

Right Grayson Perry (UK), *Art Fashion, Same Thing*.
Earthenware, 46 cm (18") ht. Collection of Elton John.

*'I long ago resigned myself to the fact that I was supplying
fragile knick-knacks for the mantle shelves of the well-to-do.
That is the nature of ceramics but I try to subvert from
within' (Grayson Perry in 'Fear and Loathing',
AN, July 1994).*

Left Kurt Weiser (USA), vessel, 1996. Whiteware, 51 cm x 28 cm (20" x 11"). Photo Noel Allum. Courtesy Garth Clark Gallery, New York.

'Obsessive, humorous, ironic, the cast porcelain teapots, plates and covered jars Weiser has made in the past four years are among the most vividly decorated forms in recent American ceramics. They are also some of the most engagingly storied. Their moral tales of scientific scrutiny, lust, predation, and godly – or worse – spousal retribution follow the thoroughly modern platonic rule that good people dream what evil people practice. There's nothing especially flashy or preachy about his pots; they simply offer the soft-spoken images of a potentially bad conscience working overtime' (Edward Lebow in 'Kurt Weiser: Storied Forms', American Craft, Dec 1994/Jan 1995).

New vessels

Whilst some favour traditional stereotypical forms as vehicles for social or formal comment, less conventional vessels have been evolving in the new ceramics of North America and Europe. The forms, freely constructed, are not classical, the surfaces no longer conventional, but they make full use of the explosion of graphic methodologies now available to the contemporary ceramist. The subject matters for surfaces are personal, observational, and make social comment.

Right Susan and Stephen Kemenyffy (USA), *Autumn Louise*. Raku sculpture, 122 cm x 76 cm x 20 cm (48" x 30" x 8").

The Kemenyffys combine new forms and a painterly development of the deeply ceramic process of raku. Stephen Kemenyffy's family was originally Hungarian, and although they deny any overt connection, there appears to be a link with the Art Nouveau of the Zsolnay ceramics produced in Pécs, Hungary in their style and the innovative adaption of lustrous raku glazes for painting.

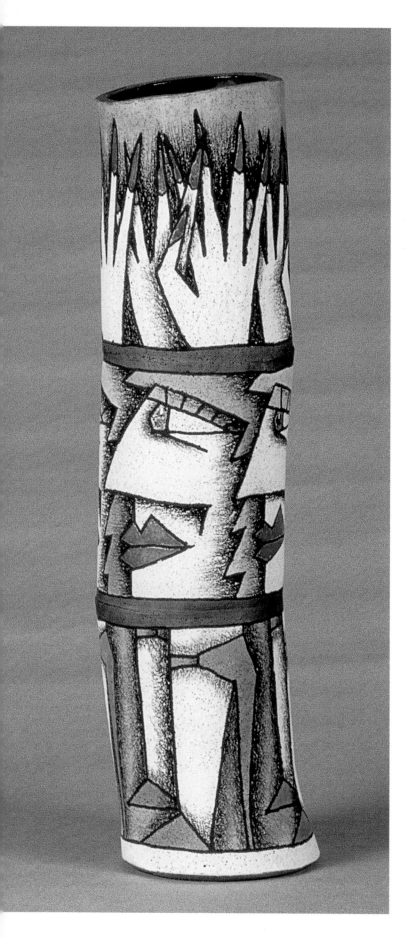

Left Rimas VisGirda (USA), small extruded cylinder, cut and reassembled – 3 sections (hands, faces, feet). Multifired. Photo Rimas VisGirda. 51 cm (20") ht.

'In the mid to late 70s I started to visit London and I went there a number of times. These travels were a visual delight, I found the Rocky Horror Show playing at a theater on Kings Road, I was intrigued by the punk movement and its visual versatility and vitality. I was delighted in all the sights and sounds so different from where I lived. I became more interested in erotica, fashion, and sub-cultures of all sorts. In particular, I remember an experience in London that persists to this day: I was on one of those very long, very steep and narrow (wooden?) escalators in the underground during rush hour; I remember looking at the escalator adjacent (going the other way) and there was this neverending parade of profiles parading across from me; each face was of course different but they were all similar. I went home and immediately drew a number of faces (profiles) on a cylinder – each similar, but each slightly different. I could rotate this pot on a turntable and I would get that same feeling as I did on the escalator watching those profiles go by. I still do that to this day and enjoy making those pieces' (Rimas VisGirda, 1988).

Left Rimas VisGirda (USA), *Cityscape,* 51 cm (20") ht, multifired. Photo Rimas VisGirda.

'A photo professor gave an assignment for his class to go out into the country with a tripod and camera, set the tripod in place and rotate the camera on the tripod so that all the photos overlap each other. These then are mounted with overlaps and result in a long 360° view of the particular setting. What I found interesting about this project / concept (which the students did not do) was that if you took the long strip of end to end photos and joined the first to the last with the image(s) to the inside and suspended the loop at eye level; you could stand inside this loop and by turning around have a truly 3-dimensional view of the particular surroundings (cut off at the top and bottom) — you therefore had a neverending piece of horizontal paper that two-dimensionally represented a three-dimensional reality (with borders top and bottom). It was not a great leap of genius to realise that such a 'system' was no more than the 'inverse' of a ceramic cylinder — and coupled with Renaissance perspective — and having to learn to draw, immediately led to numerous 'neverending' landscape drawings on pots' (Rimas VisGirda, 1988).

Above Rimas VisGirda (USA), *Cup and Saucer,* 16.5 cm x 26 cm x 26 cm (6.5" x 10" x 10"). Multifired. Photo Rimas VisGirda.

'Figure drawing gave me the idea that rather than looking "into" the pot (as in landscape), I could look at the pot and render something wrapped around the pot on the outside: a figure, which still remains a 2-dimensional representation of a 3-dimensional reality but from a different vantage point or "perspective". Next came vessels of all forms (vases, cups, teapots, etc.) "wrapped" with the female figure; singly, in pairs, and in multiples creating patterns and overlapping ... I liked the idea that the drawing represented a 3-dimensional, object, was itself 2-dimensional, but was applied to a 3-dimensional surface — sort of a dichotomy between dimensions' (Rimas VisGirda, 1988).

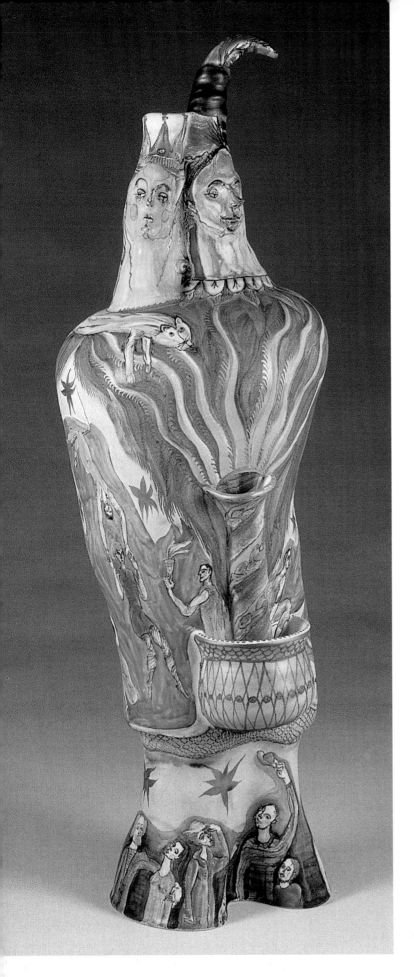

Left Simona Alexandrov (USA), *Jester Vessel*, ceramic, maiolica and lustres, 56cm (22") 1997.

Theatre is a frequent subject matter for Alexandrov. She grew up in Russia and trained in St Petersburg. At the Muchina school she came across the work and ideas of the Fauvists, Cubists, Expressionists and Constructivists, and was able to handle and study fine maiolica: 'Museum pieces are usually untouchable, you can look at them and read about them, but the chance to hold a priceless antique maiolica pot in your hands and really see how it was done was an incredible experience for me. We copied these ceramic pieces the way painting students copy the old masters — in order to experience the techniques they used and truly understand them' (Simona Alexandrov in 'Contempo-Baroque Majolica, The Art of Simona Alexandrov', by Louise Melton, in Ceramics Monthly, *May, 1996).*

Right Stephen Dixon (UK), *Bare Ladies*, 27 cm x 24 cm x 11 cm (10.5" x 9.5" x 4.5"), glazed earthenware with sprigs, monoprinting stamps enamels and lustres. Photo Stephen Dixon.

Below Stephen Dixon (UK), *Bare Ladies*, (detail). Photo Stephen Dixon.

One of the UK's 'younger generation' of ceramists who operates within a tradition of studio ceramics, but whose influences are much more eclectic and comprehensive than before. The vessels are constructed from soft slabs of 'T material' clay usually primed with a layer of coloured slip, often bearing stamped and printed imagery. Subsequent additions of slabbed and modelled figures sprigged, printed and painted marks and images complete the narrative. The pieces are multi-fired building up layers and depths of colour with coloured glazes, stains enamels and lustres' (Stephen Dixon, 1999).

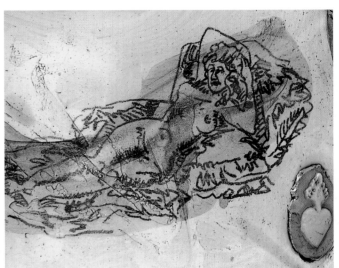

Above Les Lawrence (USA), *New Visions Vessel*, # A81202, porcelain, photo silkscreen monoprint, stainless steel, 1998.

Lawrence's use of the dollar bill, and the image of the Mona Lisa (so identified with high art) onto a form so quintessentially ceramic implies a questioning of the (ceramic) object's status in the visual arts market. The images are symbols that are part of an on-going narrative that comments on life in the late 20th century. Lawrence uses porcelain as a receptor for detailed and complex col-laged screenprinted and drawn imagery which is then used in the construction of non-functional stapled teapots and forms. Whilst some works seem to be almost random collections of found image and text, in other pieces there are clear references to particular issues. Early New Visions works juxtaposed dollar bills, printed materials and the photographic image of two white men astride the skulls and bones of hundreds of native American people. The genocide of the 19th century which helped make America wealthy is powerfully acknowledged on pieces that belong to the ceramic traditions of commemoration and political comment.

Right Linda Huey (USA), *Urban Garden*, urn on top of pedestal, low fire clay, underglaze and glaze, 144 cm x 47 cm x 47 cm (56.5" x 18.5" x 18.5") 1991.

Huey used her immediate environment as the subject matter for her painted surfaces. Beginning as a production potter painting each cup, plate and bowl, she gradually developed larger, more sculptural vases and tables, each slab-built from terracotta and covered with underglaze paintings of the city at odds with nature.

Above Stephen Benwell (Australia), large vase, handbuilt, earthenware with underglaze painting, 55 cm x 51 cm (21.5" x 21"). Photo David Macarthur.

Benwell is another painter turned potter. Although earlier work involved more complex forms and structures, and a harder graphic style of working on the surface; recent pieces are characterised by simplified forms with a painterly, expressive surface. Although he uses the pot as a canvas, he sees his work as fitting into the history of pottery rather painting. 'These works are round, continuous and not flat and so unlike a painting the image is never ending.' Indeed his glazed surfaces have a slightly dimpled, softly worked quality, and with his ambiguous personal imagery and mark making the work hints at a 'private narrative whose meaning remains elusive to the viewer' ('Stephen Benwell, Within the Tradition of Vessel Making', by Christopher Sanders in Ceramics Art and Perception, No. 27, 1997).

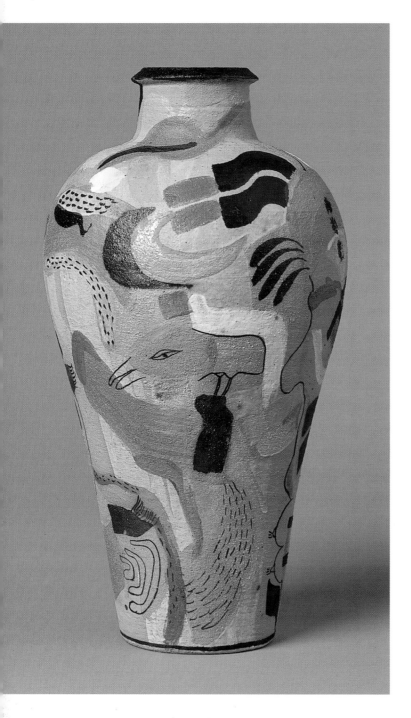

Above Herman Fogelin (Sweden), *Spring,* vase, 65 cm (25.5") ht. Slipglaze, Sur-cru. Photo Johan Hedenström.

'I have my roots in the Swedish Konstructivism, and the painter Gosta Adrian-Nilsson, active in the 1920s, has been very important to me. He wrote a book called The Divine Geometrics, *and often painted in a non-figurative manner. I hand-build my forms, I use many slipglazes and commercial colours, but I have no particular passion for firing and kilns, rather I see the kiln as a kind of washing machine, you put your work in, it does its work and after a couple of hours its ready to open.'*

Right George Schwarzbach (Germany), *Baroque Vase with Flower Strips,* 40 cm (16"), in and overglaze painting on stoneware.

Another painter influenced by the baroque forms and colours of Bavaria, and the Mediterranean tradition of maiolica: 'Human beings are always the theme of my ceramic paintings. The figures appear full of passion and pain, often wanting to free themselves from their fate (I use bridges, ladders, planes and other symbols suggesting this).'

Left Thomas Kerrigan (USA), *Spirit Realm A–VI*, porcelain with black slip, sgraffito, 60 cm (24") ht. 1994.

'My involvement with these works is intuitive in character, forms and imagery emerge and merge fluidly.'

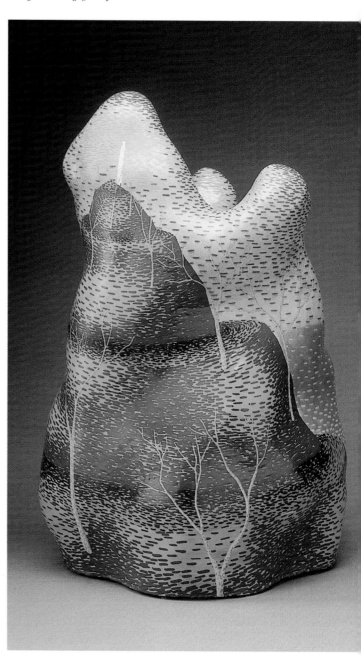

Above Mic Stowell (USA), *Floating Cowboys*, 63 cm x 41 cm x 46 cm (25" x 16" x 18"), 1988. Terracotta clay, painted underglaze and glaze, 1988.

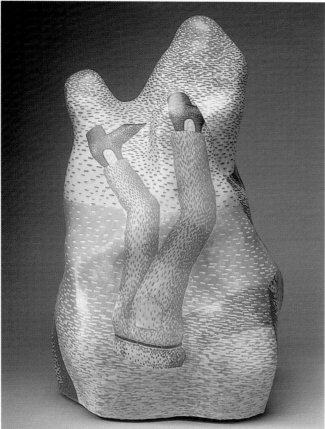

Left Mic Stowell (USA), *Floating Cowboys*, alternate view, 63 cm x 41 cm x 46 cm (25" x 16" x 18"). Terracotta clay, painted underglaze and glaze, 1988.

Right Sandra Taylor (Australia), *Final Merger, View 1*, 60 cm x 30 cm (24" x 12").

Hand-built, painted with underglaze colours, overpainting and multi-fired to achieve surface layering of colour. From the beginning, she 'fought to escape the stranglehold of the Bernard Leach tradition', narrating human folly and the struggle to manage lives where dreams and realities seldom mesh. With her own brand of dark humour her painting on vessels and forms 'allows the drama to be played out on all sides'. (Quotes from 'Romantic Dividends, New Works by Sandra Taylor', by Helen Stephens, in Ceramics Art and Perception, *No. 24, 1996)*

Left Matt Nolen (USA),
Love Tower, porcelain, 1996.
76 cm x 38 cm (30" x 15").
Courtesy Garth Clark Gallery.
Photo D. James Dee.

*A contemporary tulip vase, made up
of four separate forms. Painting refers
to different kinds and stages of love.
From the physical and erotic, to the
tender, companionable and self-love.
Matt Nolen is amongst a new
generation of artists who are working
graphically with the vessel and its
surface. Originally trained as a
painter and architect, he found the
restrictions of conventional painting
ultimately unsatisfying, and
discovered that ceramics offered the
possibility of 'painting in the round'.*

*In 1990 after one of Nolen's friends
died of Aids, he found a new urgency
to life, and began to use serious topics
in his forms, and the imagery painted
upon them. His treatment of subjects
is subtle, the pieces don't shout at
you, the form and painting intrigue,
and invite you in before the message
hits. His forms are hand-built, and
whilst they make reference to
convention, they are idiosyncratic
fantasies; a winged angel in a
pin-striped suit stands atop a* Credit
Card Reliquary Jar, *doffed hands
emerge handle like on the shoulder of
the* Glitter and be Gay *palace vase.*

Right *Plate Painted with a View of
Arras.* Soft paste porcelain, paint-
ed in enamel colours and gilt.
Tournai Belgium, c. 1780.
24 cm (9.5") dia. Courtesy of
The Bowes Museum, Barnard
Castle, Co. Durham.

CHAPTER 7

2D/3D . . . Trompe l'oeil, Relief and Sculpture

Trompe l'oeil

Vessels provide interesting canvases, but painting and drawing realistic perspective on flat and curved ceramic surfaces have long caused logistical problems for ceramic painters. They also create rich possibilities, not only in the trick of the eye created by painting, but also by the judicious use of modelling and working the surface. There is a tradition of trompe l'oeil ceramics in Europe that can be traced back at least as far as the 16th-century work of Bernard Palissy, and probably even further.

Above Kevin Petrie (UK), *Paris in Springtime,* onglaze screen print on bone china (reduced solvent waterbased ceramic transfer system), 1998, edition of 6.

This piece has an image of masking tape, to create the trompe l'oeil effect of the print being stuck on the ware. 'It makes reference to 18th-century ware which used similar devices, and also acknowledges that transfers are separate from the ware and form an added layer of meaning.' (Kevin Petrie 1998).

Right Anne Kraus (USA), *Lost Dream Tile.* 84 cm x 66 cm (33" x 26"), whiteware, painted underglaze and glaze. Photo Noel Allum. Courtesy Garth Clark Gallery, New York. Text reads: It becomes necessary to let the wind blow though the building — to relieve the pressure so that the very walls are not blown in. And what had seemed a concrete path of achievement turns instead to fragments that contain dreams and half forgotten memories.

Originally a painter in New York City, Kraus switched her attentions to ceramics after a period of infatuation with china painted porcelains. 'One thing that distinguishes ceramics for me, and which never happened with painting, is that I tumbled head over heels into it. It was like being swept up in a huge wave. My feeling for ceramic history, for ceramic tradition, is a great love. I see something that I find so beautiful and I just want to make my version of it. It is a gift, a payment that I make to the tradition' (Anne Kraus). Although she has worked cups, teapots and vases ('I have seen grown men pale at the sight of one of Anne Kraus's teacups', Garth Clark), her most recent work has been trompe l'oeil panels, where she extends the environment her art inhabits.

'It's like a pot with a dream in it that is sitting inside of a dream. A dream within a dream.' Her subjects are vaguely obscure, dreamlike and surrealist... 'a trafficking in symbol and metaphor. One reads them first and then passes through the drawings into landscapes and events.' (Quotes from Garth Clark and Anne Kraus in Anne Kraus a Survey, catalogue, for exhibition at Garth Clark gallery 1998.)

Above Deborah Black (Canada), *Fruit Bowl (teal),* 1996, shown resting on its rim.

'The fruit bowls are three-dimensional, the interior of which is painted to resemble a bowl containing fruit. The still-life creates the illusion, a trompe l'oeil effect, so that when the bowl is stood on its rim, it looks like a bowl full of fruit. Resting on its foot ring, the bowl serves as such and may be used to hold fruit. Intense colours are achieved by traditional painting technique of overlaying various colours of slip to create a sense of depth and chiaroscuro. Finally, clear and coloured transparent glazes added to the surface further this dimensional effect. These pieces function in a dual sense: as still-life paintings and as bowls full of fruit.'

Below Deborah Black (Canada), *Fruit Bowl (teal),* 1996, 40 cm x 12 cm (15.75" x 4.5"), earthenware, slips, glazes, shown resting on its foot ring.

Above Doug Baldwin (USA), *Duck Art Revisited, Towards Abstraction,* after
Vasilii Kandinsky, ceramic, painted onglaze enamels 28 cm x 38 cm (11" x
15"), 1996.

Above Pablo Picasso: *Still Life with Six Fish and a Slice of Lemon,* Louis XV plate, white earthenware, modelled elements applied, incised, painted with oxides and slips, glazed. 23 cm (9"). Undated 1953. Photo Courtesy Images Modernes.

Right Doug Baldwin (USA), *Duck Art Revisited, The Melancholy mystery of a Street,* after De Chirico, ceramic, underglaze pencil earthenware, 28 cm x 28 cm (11" x 15 ") 1966.

'For the past twenty years I've been making clay ducks. I call them ducks because of their beaks. They have always taken many forms, but humour has always been an important element.'

The super realism of Richard Shaw, Victor Spinski and others is another type of trompe l'oeil, exclusively ceramic and dealing with three dimensional sculpture, and super 'real', ceramic surface.

Top left Juris Bergins (Latvia), *Teapot, with Myself and Grandfather*, bone china, overglaze painting, 30 cm x 30 cm x 9 cm (12" x 12" x 3.5"). Photo Zivile Barzilauskaite.

Bergins' surreal forms and assemblages are sculptural, painted trompe l'oeil. He produces a deeply personal and narrative expression, often political in motive and intent.

Left Victor Spinski (USA), *Giving up Painting its too Messy*, 1998. 36 cm x 41 cm x 24 cm (14" x 16" x 9.5"), from Clay Realists, at the Nancy Margolis Gallery. Low fire clay and glazes, lustre and direct photo transfer of Coca Cola image on box.

Super realism is still alive and well. 'My work is highly technical ceramics created in trompe l'oeil style. The subject matter I mostly deal with is social commentary with some degree of dark humour and violence. My art has a lot to do with American culture, which I portray as merchants of mediocrity and consumption. I enjoy creating works of various situations that delve into the psychological profile of different individuals. Some of my clay art objects lament the passing of personal touch and craftsmanship of everyday objects that would enhance the quality of our life. I don't think of myself as a harbinger of doom: I only want to remind the viewer that quality might be more interesting then quantity' (Victor Spinski, 1999).

Right Juris Bergins (Latvia), Teapot, bone china, overglaze painting. Photo Zivile Barzilauskaite.

Above Mishima Kimiyo (Japan), *Copy 82*. Ceramic, silk screen, paper. Yamaguchi Prefectural Museum of Art (1980–1982).

Installation with paper, and ceramic boxes, magazines, newspapers and leaflets. Japanese ceramics are not all tea bowls and wood fire. For Mishima, ceramics is not an end in itself. 'I aim for ceramic works without even the slightest trace of being made from ceramics,' Mishima Kimiyo, in 'The Meeting of Ceramics and Printed Matter', by Suzuki Kenji, in Ceramics Art and Perception, *No. 25, 1996.*

Right Paul Scott (UK), *Surplus Fabrics*, 1985, 28 cm x 38 cm (11" x 15"). Photo Andrew Morris.

Bas relief… 'A natural effect of drawing into soft clay is the relief qualities thrown up by marking a line. Later as the clay dries its characteristics change and it is possible to carve into and build upon the surface. At biscuit you have a monochromatic image in relief, which is then enhanced and completed by painting, in this case in underglaze colours and body stains. This small shop was changed dramatically for the worse, soon after this work was made. The characteristic brickwork associated with the Carlisle area of North Cumbria was covered in cement render, and the whole facade painted white, effectively destroying the original character and value of the building's appearance. Ironically, as well as in the work itself, the image of the building lives on, in several thousand postcards which have sold over the years.'

Relief

Carved wooden and stone reliefs have often been employed architecturally, particularly in churches and on public buildings and terracotta versions are a common feature of some Victorian architecture, but the use of clay surface relief by artists, used in conjunction with painting, perhaps landscape and figurative, also has an unsettling effect on the eye, and is in an area that is in a virtual 'no man's land'. Unloved by potters, avoided by others, it is apparently a problematic area of study, but one of intrigue, interest and possibilities. Shearer West's *A Guide to Art* defines relief as 'A sculptural design which extends out from a flat surface, but which is not freestanding. There are several different levels of relief: *Alto-rilievo*, or high relief, *mezzo-rilievo*, medium relief and *bas relief* or low relief. *Rilievo shiacciato* is the most shallow relief of all and approximates most closely to two-dimensional media.'

Little appears to have been written about ceramic reliefs, although like trompe l'oeil, they have a long history and tradition.

Below *Stigmatisation of St. Francis.* Relief plaque. Painted tin-glazed earthenware, 24.5 x 29 cm (9.5" x 11.5"). Florence, Italy (workshop of the Della Robbia family), c. 1500. X1560 The Bowes Museum, Barnard Castle, Co. Durham.

Right György Kungl (Hungary), *The American Embassy in Rome,* 1992, porcelain relief with underglaze painting, 30 cm x 30 cm x 97 cm (12" x 12" x 38").

Kungl has consistently worked in relief, and ceramic sculpture, and seems to move effortlessly between the two. The painted surface is a vital constituent of the work.

Below right György Kungl (Hungary), *Presso,* porcelain relief with engobe painting, 40 cm x 54 cm x 20 cm (16" x 21" x8").

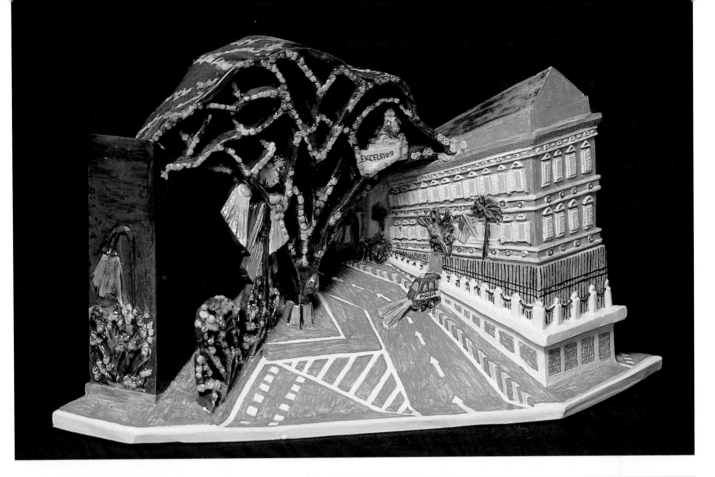

Jan Holcomb's use of oil paints instead of ceramic colours on sculptural reliefs is not that unusual. The painter Jack Earl is another who works in this way. In the UK, George Walker's technically similar work also has a singularly nightmarish quality to it, but Walker's pieces are freestanding sculptures.

Right Jan Holcomb (USA), *Three States*, 1990. Stoneware and oil paint. 89 cm x 60 cm x 25 cm (35" x 24" x 10"). Photo Paul Roselli.

Holcomb describes his works as 'dimensional paintings'. Early wall pieces were framed between heavy clay columns and pediments suggesting obelisks or gateways made from logs, but an evolution of imagery and content has led the pieces to be more individually free, the image 'framing itself'.

'Holcomb's big headed, cartoonish figures set in a dream world of stylised landscapes, may seem whimsical at first. But on closer examination, the seriousness of what they represent becomes apparent. Through the narrative implied by the scenes he depicts, Holcomb describes to us the fears and pressures of living in the nuclear age, in an uncertain toxic world of increasing limitations and depleted resources' (M. F. Porges from 'Children of an Anxious Age' American Ceramics 6/4).

Left Jan Holcomb (USA), *Reorientation*, 1988. Stoneware and oil paint. 92 cm x 60 cm x 25 cm (35" x 24" x 10"). Photo Barnaby Evans.

'A wild-eyed man perches precariously on the roof of a skewed house. Before him a row of gravestones lines a road, echoed by a facing line of trees. Tiny figures twist in the spokes of an astronomy zodiac wheel spread across the sky behind him, as if blown far out into the atmosphere. The explosive energy of this image describes the nuclear holocaust — the worst nightmare of a generation that grew up during the Cold War, hiding under desks during bomb drills wondering each time: Is this the way the world will end?' (M. F. Porges 'Children of an Anxious Age' American Ceramics 6/4).

Above George Walker (UK), *The Arms Dealer,* 44 cm x 42 cm x 20 cm (17.5" x 16.5" x 8"). 1995. Teapot, earthenware and paint. Photo courtesy Dr Maureen Michaelson.

The dealer sits astride a tank with a missile in a pocket, another in one hand, a bottle of booze in the other. His female persona (the handle) is bound and blindfolded. On top of her a soldier carries a flag, one side of which reads 'if not us, others' referring to the excuses Western governments use in selling arms to unstable regimes. The head of the arms dealer with its cigar puffing mouth is the lid of the teapot, the gun barrel the spout.

'Walker's images are like our worst nightmares, but a nightmare is a transitory phenomenon, glimpsed and then gone, much to the relief of the dreamer. Walker fixes these moments of heightened insight permanently rock solid in clay. He allows no texture in his work, his colours are garish and uniformly applied. Texture would provide an opportunity for the eye to pause, a moment in which the vision might go out of focus' (Pamela Johnston, October 1989).

Left Patti Warashina (USA), *Wash N'Wear*, 71 cm x 46 cm x 36 cm (28" x18" x 14"). Clay, glaze and underglaze. Photo Rodger Schreiber.

'Many of my sculptural ideas stem from painting, perhaps because clay surface must be addressed as a three-dimensional canvas, even after the form is built. Early on, I was intrigued by the Surrealists, many of whom worked representationally. At that time, the most experimental and progressive work in clay was being done on the West Coast. I thought about artists like Voulkos, Takamoto, Price and Arneson, as well as some of my instructors whose work I admired, even though I was in Seattle, and outside the movement. My ideas were inspired by the visceral and human emotions of their work, but I also continued to look at painting for literal content and color ....

Over the years, I have found that dealing with the figure has allowed me to explore the idiosyncrasies and foibles of human nature, in which I have always been in wonder and fascination' (Patti Warashina 1998).

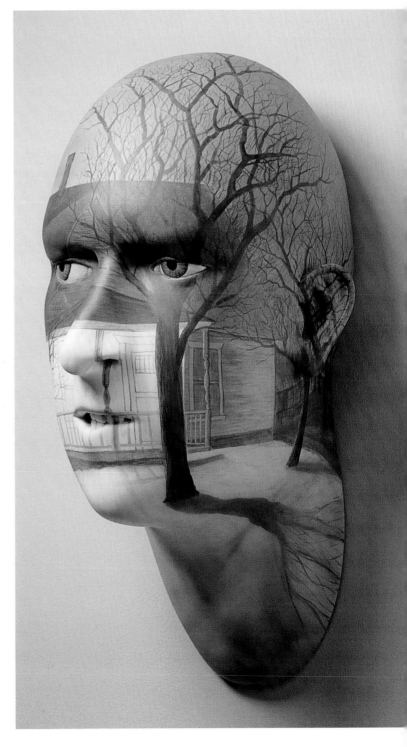

Below John Woodward (USA), *Front Porch.* Painted ceramic, 56 cm x 30 cm x 30 cm (22" x 12" x 12"), 1996, A fusion of the classic precepts of portrait, bust, and landscape painting. Photo Tim Thayer.

'The heads are perfectly smooth and hairless and the individual characteristics of the face and chest are achieved through the modelling of clay. The nose and lips and ears are not painted as facial features, but serve as a backdrop for a landscape or cityscape. The eyes of these figures are the only portion of the portrait that is painted, with the rest of the bust given over to larger overall painting.'

Above Ralph Bacerra (USA), *Portrait Vessel, 1994.* Whiteware, 89 cm x 49 cm (35" x 19"). Photo Anthony Cunha. Courtesy Garth Clark Gallery.

A one-time student of Howard Kottler, and identified with others including Adrian Saxe in a movement referred to as 'fetish finish'. The movement demanded a style of flawlessly constructed work, with seductive surface design and form. Although now distancing himself somewhat from association with this style, Bacerra still places importance on its underlying assumptions: 'Technique is a high priority. The skill has to be evident in each piece. That is to say that the form should be pleasing, the glaze and colours are right and the design is completely worked out. If these elements are not in place, then I am not satisfied with the work …'

'I am not making any statements — social, political, conceptual or even intellectual. There is no meaning or metaphor. I am committed more to the idea of pure beauty. When it is finished, the piece should be like an ornament, exquisitely beautiful' (Ralph Bacerra quoted in article by Jo Lauria, 'Ralph Bacerra, Ceramic Artist' in Ceramics Art and Perception *No. 15, 1994).*

Above Michael Gross (USA), *Untitled*, 61 cm x 25 cm (24" x 10"). Clay, iron and stone. Photo courtesy of Ann Nathan Gallery Chicago.

Above Michael Gross (USA), *Table*. Photo courtesy of Ann Nathan Gallery, Chicago.

Dark and intriguing, Michael Gross's ceramics recall African masks and carvings, but his subject matter records middle class, Midwestern America. 'The figures that populate Gross's work are as entangled and contorted as the stories they tell. Gross obsessively fills every inch of his work with images, creating a tumultuous orgy in which hidden figures emerge between arms and legs.' (Angela Kramer Murphy in 'The Seven Deadly Sins Meet Main Street' Ceramics Art and Perception, No.12, 1993.)

Left Neil Brownsword (UK), *Not Tonight*. Ceramic collage with found objects, 85 cm x 43 cm x 41 cm (33" x 17" x 16").

Brownsword collages three dimensionally, with painted underglaze, glaze and graphic details produced with decals. Industrially-produced figurines never looked like this, but there is something of the tradition here, for Brownsword grew up in Stoke-on-Trent, England's industrial ceramic heartland. His work is ruthlessly autobiographical, coming from personal experiences of life as a young man in the relentlessly unforgiving 1990s.

'Brownsword makes things that are frequently about sex, doubt and instability, which are explicit without crudity; revelations in clay that balance humour and the grotesque, with intimacy and his certain touch with materials' (Alison Britton in 'Neil Brownsword, the Fine Line', Revelations in Clay, catalogue for exhibition/residency at the City Museum and Art gallery, Stoke-on-Trent 1996).

Above Viola Frey (USA), *Reclining Nude*, 1995, 77 cm x 29 cm x 56 cm (30.5" x 11.5" x 22"). Photo courtesy Rena Bransten Gallery, San Francisco.

Frey first used clay in the early 1950s, its three dimensional qualities particularly appealed, but she also perceived that clay could unify 'all the resources of drawing, of painting of color, light, gloss, matt of solids of space'. Towards the end of the 1960s, she 'began polychroming her clay sculpture. The effect was to diminish the inherent three-dimensionality of her medium, bringing the sculpture closer to her concurrent painting and drawing' (Patterson Sims from 'Viola Frey at the Whitney', in Ceramics Monthly *November, 1984).*

'I enjoy working with the nude. Its a timeless subject matter. Because they are glazed and painted they don't really appear to be naked in the same way as the French Salon or cleaned up Greek sculptures. If they are about seduction, they are not so pornographic as the all white' (Viola Frey quoted in Ceramic Review, *157, 1996).*

Right Jeff Irwin (USA), *Nest*, earthenware, black underglaze, wax resist and sgraffito. 76 cm x 56 cm x 30 cm (30" x 22" x 12"). Photo Jeff Irwin.

'I develop a narrative by placing symbols in juxtaposition with their origins, or in otherwise ironic settings. This conflict between expectation and contradiction is further reinforced by the placement of the drawings on sculptural forms. In one area the sculptural character may be defined and strengthened by the drawings, in other areas the form itself may be nullified …. I spent my graduate years moving back and forth between building three dimensional images and drawing two dimensional images, never willing to give up either for a single focus. Then by accident, or desperation, I began putting drawings on my ceramic sculpture. This seemed to fulfil the need for both dimensions.'

Above left Maria Geszler (Hungary), *Rousseau's Garden,* porcelain figure, silk screen print, salt kiln, wood-fired, 1300°C, 79 cm x 34 cm x 15 cm (31" x 13.5" x 6") 1980.

Above right Maria Geszler (Hungary), *Poetry of the Industrial Landscape,* porcelain figure, silk screen print, salt kiln, wood-fired, 1300°C, 80 cm x 36 cm x 16 cm (31.5" x 14" x 6.5"), 1990.

Geszler has long combined the graphic and the ceramic; silk screen printing is an essential element of her porcelain sculptures which are subjected to high fire wood and salt kilns work to achieve the particular balance of glaze and colour that she requires.

'Kaput the fingers
and the bone.
Writing the poems
and hearing the music.

Life is running,
in my dreams,
Mozart,
Beethoven,
Nuclear power stations.

Flying the metals and
the smoke together.
Folding together the figures.

Windows,
surrealistic pictures
and Andy Warhol.

Chamber orchestras
and white flutes
Blindfold figures,
solitary benches and
Rousseau's garden.

Utamaro,
wood cuts and industry.

Graphical parts and
sculptural parts and
shadows.

Ceramic...
It is from painting,
It is from Sculpture...'

('Maria Geszler, Poet of the
Industrial Landscape',
Paul Scott, 1998.)

Right Jindra Viková (Czech Republic), *Portrait of someone unknown*. Porcelain and metal, 36 cm x 32 cm (14" x 12.5"), 1983.

Vikova's work has long straddled the sculptural and the graphic. Working with thin slabs of fine porcelain she constructs animated portrait silhouettes. Drawing on specific reservoirs of memory, or an individual, known face, she creates in a fragile substance the moment of a fleeting facial expression, which is later fixed permanently by fire. Juxtaposed with judiciously splashed slips, her painting and drawing with paintbrush and underglaze colour is fine and subtle.

'She captures a facet of affectation, an involuntary state of mind, shy or with a self-satisfied suggestion of a smile, as well as an expression of fear... The completion of the silhouette happens in the heat of the furnace. Here the thin leaves bend somewhat more, each personality comes to its characteristic movement, as though it is a real creature with a certain way of behaviour in real space. In the heat of the furnace each silhouette takes on its own individual shape so that as a certain character it enters directly on the stage of life' (Jindra Viková, Benice Spa Publishing, Prague 1997).

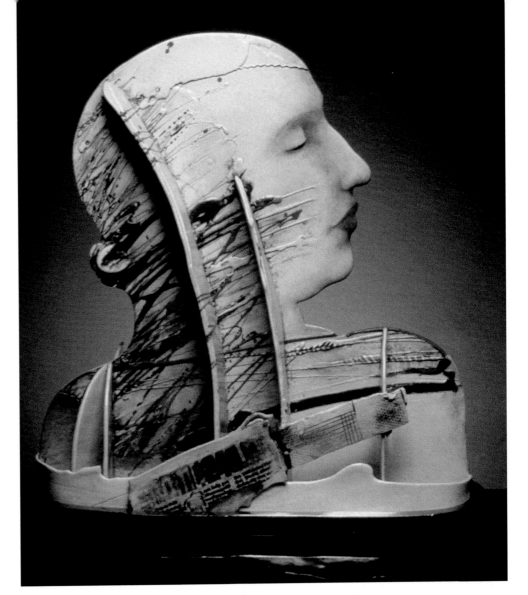

Right Rimas VisGirda (USA), *Three in a Row*. Sculpture, multi-fire, 13 cm x 30 cm x 10 cm (5" x 12" x 4"). Photo Rimas VisGirda.

'In the mid to late 80s I also started to make sculpture ... up until this time my work was committed primarily to vessels with only a few diversions. Working sculpturally (mostly busts and heads) was interesting because I could choose to make certain projections (i.e. noses) in the round and simply draw others (i.e. ears) onto the surface and with shading I could cause a confusion with what was actually in the round and what was 2 dimensional. I like the 'illusion' or 'caricature' of dimensions and use shadows (drawn) and shading to add a certain visual confusion to my work' (Rimas VisGirda 1998).

CHAPTER 8

Plates, Prints, Words, Photographs and Tiles

The plate

The plate or shallow bowl (apart from the tile) is perhaps the most accessible ceramic form for artists from other media to paint, print and draw on and is also a favourite canvas for those whose main medium is the ceramic. After all, it effectively offers a flat plain with circular frame, not complicated by continuous surfaces, or insides and outsides. The lack of volume and apparent ease of use alienates the plate from the discourse of those concerned primarily with the vessel as object. It is true that as a form it has meaning in its use for food, but it also has an historical role as a picture plain, a wall piece, and here it is far too close for comfort to the flatness of paintings, prints or drawings on paper. For those who see ceramics as 'forever a form', the wish to maintain a discrete distance and separate identity is under threat in the plate's function in this role.

Howard Kottler, explaining the difficulties he had with his work on plates said: 'In ceramics you are supposed to attack the form and surface as a total entity. But in this case I wasn't interested in form. I used the same commercial blanks over and over again, like blank canvases. So the plates didn't meet certain standards of the ceramics world' [55].

Another good example of the virtual blind spot that writers on the applied and decorative arts have here is

Richard Slee who is well-known for his earthenware sculptural objects, which reference ceramic ornament as found in the English suburban home. He has also produced printed plates and shallow bowls, which examine the simple and humble ceramic tradition of block printing with the same wry humour. These pieces are much less well-known.

[55] in *Howard Kottler Face to Face*, Patricia Failing, University of Washington Press 1995.

142

Right Karen Densham (UK), *Boy, Dog/Girl, Cat*, earthenware, poured slip, bleeding oxide, monoprint, impressed text, 45 cm (18") dia., 1996.

Karen Densham has been producing hand-built plates since the mid-1980s. Peter Dormer observed, 'her plates have an individual quality of paintings ... they are poignant, they suggest the struggle to hold on to the memory of something or someone that is valuable... Densham wants to make plates that have poetry' (Crafts Magazine, No. 12, 1993). This work depicts two Staffordshire figures which reminded her 'of the amusing way in which certain animals are personified as either male or female'.

Left Richard Slee (UK), *Fruit Machine Plate*. Earthenware, with screenprinted decals and rubber stamp border.

Writing about his investigation into low tech printing processes for studio ceramics, Slee says: 'Part of my motivation was a reaction to the state of decoration and image-making in contemporary ceramics, which I felt lacked meaning, depth and creativity. I wished to address these issues and also attempt to create a relationship between shape and image that was equal and flexible' (Richard Slee in 'Reinventing the Familiar', from Hot off the Press, Ceramics and Print, *Bellew 1996*).

Right Viola Frey (USA), *Woman with a Polka Dot Dress*, ceramic, 66 cm x 15 cm (26" x 6"). Photo courtesy Rena Bransten Gallery, San Francisco.

'Frey's plates reveal her bricoleur's ability to fashion something from odds and ends. These non-functional plates cannot be classified as either traditional painting or sculpture. The vessel has turned pictorial and its narrative, like its circular border, flows inconclusively. Using replica bric a brac objects Frey concocts from the trite a complex cultural narrative' (Patterson Sims from 'Viola Frey at the Whitney', in Ceramics Monthly, November, 1984).

Plates have long depicted the political, and the gory. In 1998, the tradition of depicting the grisly, is still alive and well. In 1989 Seattle artist Charles Krafft (painting self proclaimed 'savage surrealist fresco paintings' without a great deal of critical attention) made contact with one of his boyhood heroes, the originator of custom car pinstriping, Von Dutch. The ensuing correspondence and collaboration between the two led Krafft to produce a portrait of the pinstriper in Delft-style blue and white. In order to do the work he had to learn the art of china painting: 'The winter I spent sitting in with the venerable dames of the Northwest china painters changed the course of my career forever.' With his 'sagacious blue-haired grannies' Krafft 'diligently mastered' the daintiness of the Delft style, but once home, replaced the windmills, duck ponds and ruminating cows of Holland with the 1945 bombing of Dresden, Los Angeles riots, derailed trains and car accidents, nuclear mushroom clouds, tornadoes and other equally disturbing and catastrophic events.

Above Plate, *The Execution of Louis XVI.* Tin-glazed earthenware. 22 cm (8.5") dia., French (Nevers), 1793. The Bowes Museum, Barnard Castle, Co. Durham.

Left Charles Krafft, *Disasterware* (USA), *Wah Mee Club Massacre,* onglaze china painting used on restaurant plate, 26 cm (10") dia. Collection of Richard Gold.

Shortly before midnight on Feb 18 1983, three young, armed men entered the historic Wah Mee gambling club in Seattle's downtown. When they walked away, they left 14 people dead and pocketed tens of thousands of dollars in cash. It was the worst massacre in Seattle's history. The plate used by Krafft is from the Kau Kau restaurant in the same street, just opposite the (now closed) Wah Mee club. 'I'm making fun of a tradition of ceramics that's been around since the 16th century and satirising it for immediate impact. What I am doing with Disasterware is pure kitsch, a cheap souvenir. This is 'low brow' art, like skateboard designs and Pop Art. It's not Abstract 'high art' which doesn't register with people' (Charles Krafft 1995).

Above Charles Krafft, *Disasterware* (USA), *Dutch Schultz, Beer Baron of the Bronx*, tile diptych, cobalt underglaze on stoneware.

Dutch Schultz was a famous American gangster from the Al Capone era (1930s). His birth and death dates are recorded in the piece. He was shot by a rival gangster. 'I did four pictures (eight tiles altogether) of the death of Dutch Schultz, the one of him bleeding on a cafe table is No. 2 in the series.'

Right *Mission to Slovenia* advert:
'*Collectors plates are something we've all seen in souvenir shops, or advertised on the back pages of supermarket tabloids and Sunday papers. After wading through the usual swill of bad news and lurid gossip you can usually find one of these limited editions of a maudlin portrait or a rhapsodic pastoral to send away for. We never find pictures of the gritty life most of us are living in the late 20th century on ornamental china because no one wants to hang it on their walls, much less eat off it ... The daintiness of the Delft tradition lent itself nicely to the detailed depiction of the natural and sociopolitical catastrophes I wanted to commemorate. Of course this Darkness in Delft won't appeal to everyone, but if Von Dutch's enthusiasm and the discreet approval of the sagacious grannies who taught me how to do this counts, then as long as I enjoy and am learning from it, whatever I paint upon a plate must be right*' (Charles Krafft, 1995).

Above Greg Bell and Michael Keighery (Australia), *Stockmarket plate,* printed clay, jigger jollied to make plate, earthenware, 40 cm (16") dia.

(*'Curiously prophetic of stockmarkets in turmoil?',* Studio Pottery, *34, 1998).*

Above George Bowes (USA), *Pump up the Ongoing Assault,* painted underglaze on porcelain, 30 cm (12") dia., 1995. Photo Daniel Milner.

'Using porcelain, Bowes makes functional objects then embellishes the surfaces with painted images and messages intended to make the viewer think about the often violent and prejudiced nature of contemporary society.'

Left Greg Bell and Michael Keighery (Australia), *Pope platter,* printed clay, jigger jollied to make plate, earthenware, 40 cm (16") dia., 1994.

Bell, a painter and printmaker, has been working with ceramics in recent years. These pieces were produced at the University of Western Sydney Macarthur Centre for Ceramic Research, Australia.

Top right Paul Scott (UK), *The Scott Collection Cumbrian Blue(s) (Seascale Pigeon) 7/3/1.* Collaged screen printed decals in cobalt blue on Royal Worcester bone china plate with gold rim, 25 cm (10") dia., 1998. Photo Andrew Morris. Collaged from photocopies of old engravings, some altered and drawn into.

In February 1998 pigeons roosting at the Sellafield nuclear site in Cumbria, England were found to carry levels of radiation which were described by British Nuclear Fuels Limited as 'significant'. Some of the birds were roosting in the nearby village of Seascale .... Later Dr Helen Wallace of Greenpeace asked, 'How can BNFL pretend that they have their plutonium factory under control when they have nuclear waste flying over the fence?' All the local pigeons were subsequently culled.

Right Paul Scott (UK), *The Scott Collection, Cumbrian Blue(s) (Seascale Pigeon).* Screen print, decal in cobalt blue on Royal Worcester bone china plate with platinum rim, 25 cm (10") dia. 1999. Photo Andrew Morris. Digitally altered photographs, collaged with scanned and digitally manipulated old engravings.

Collaging initially with paper and photocopies has led to more sophisticated image manipulation on on a Macintosh computer. The computer offers endless possibilities... Scanned contemporary photographs are first digitally manipulated to create engravings or mezzotints, and are then combined with scanned old engravings. This is a more fluid and intuitive way of working than paper collaging (although the latter can also be employed after printing out). The direct outputting of digital image from computer to film preserves resolution and leads to even finer print quality.

'Plates have long had a role in commemoration; whilst I realise my subject matters do not always make for comfortable viewing, there is an extraordinary beauty in these monumental industrial plants. The plates celebrate this beauty as well as alluding to the follies of human arrogance towards the environment.'

Krafft is not alone in his use of the blue and white plate to commemorate the less savoury aspects of contemporary society.

Hugo Kaagman, a self taught artist in Amsterdam, has worked variously as a spray can artist on the streets, producer of his own magazine, and muralist in Amsterdam city centre. In 1988 he began to shape his canvasses either square or circular like Delft tiles and plates. He used them initially as a vehicle for ironic commentary on political or current events, but more recently his work has evolved to become less satirical and more affectionate. 'Originally it was intended as a parody of the Dutch culture and all its corny landmarks, but gradually it turned into a romantic image of the Netherlands, with kitsch features as well as symbols. Tribal motifs from the Land of the Nether are mixed into one·big Dutch party: a pure candlelight and power of folk lore reinstated into these post-modern times.' Kaagman designed the Dutch blue and white tail for the British Airways jumbo jet liveries, which Lady Thatcher so infamously derided.

The Museum Het Kruithuis' in its active role of collecting ceramics by painters, is an indication of an ongoing dialogue between fine artists and ceramists in Holland. Another is the Kunst in Keramiek (KIK) foundation which aims to provide artists other than ceramists with the opportunity to work with ceramics.

Above Hugo Kaagman (Netherlands), *Nether Art or Kaagware: Nether Art,* underglaze stencilled plate, 35 cm (14") dia.

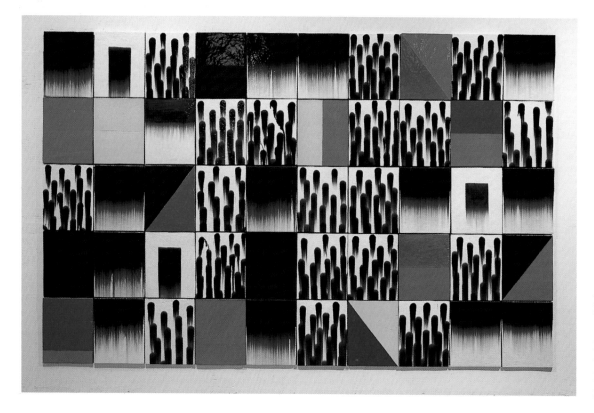

Left Jun Kaneko (USA), *Untitled,* painting in glaze and underglaze 370 cm x 232.5 cm (12 x 7.6') European Ceramics workcentre. 1996. Photo Takashi Hatakeyama.

Right Hugo Kaagman (Netherlands), *Nether Art or Kaagware: Deanware*, underglaze stencilled plate, 35 cm (14") dia.

'In recent years we have grown accustomed to seeing either no decoration or very simple decoration in paintings and pottery. Modern plastic surfaces tend to be patterned with abstract designs or texture effects. We have tended to forget that decoration can also contain figures, patterns and symbols that mean something; we need reminding that ornament can have themes. After so much brush-and-drab work it is therefore refreshing to see ornament by Hugo Kaagman. In particular, he knows that decoration can be used to tell a story, without being narrative. He uses images that everyone can understand. By drawing the inspiration from consumerism he subverts it by mocking its packaging and style both as an ornamentalist and as a commentator. The times we live in are still shot through with an ambivalence about decoration to a point that it is almost a guilty affair. But in the case of Kaagman we can read new ornament two ways at once; as decoration in its own right, and as a commentary, a reflection upon the ornamental excess of the past. This way we can speak of an ironic ornamentalist. There has to be a degree of invention in the absence of a shared system of belief. In fact the use by ceramists of art-historical references may be the closest the modern artist can come to finding imagery that a number of people can understand, simply because art history and the museums industry are almost the new 'religion' of our time; especially since museums have become de facto churches (and churches have become de facto museums)' (Dr Jeannette Dekeukeleire writing about work done by Kaagman at the European Ceramic Work Centre, s'Hertogenbosch, Netherlands).

Right KIK, Roland Sips (Netherlands), *Untitled*, painting in cobalt, 50 cm (19.5") dia.

Traditional print and the surface

The rise in interest in the relationship of ceramics and fine art printmaking has led a number of artists to research and use particular print processes or approaches to the surface.

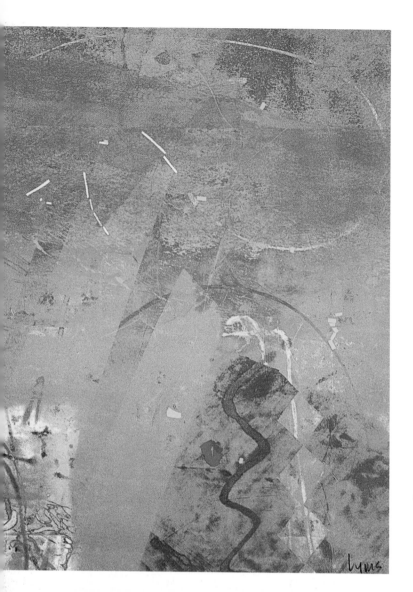

Left Mitch Lyons (USA), *Albany,* slip clay monoprint, on paper, 63 cm x 48 cm (25" x 19").

Lyons uses clay, not as the base for his prints, but as the medium. He prints off a large slab of moist clay, which has been worked with slips stained by organic and inorganic pigments. The resulting (dried) prints are framed and handled in exactly the same way as other prints on paper. 'Many ceramic techniques can be applied to the slab, such as slip trailing, stamping and incising to provide texture and colour. I know of no other printing process that allows you to manipulate the plate surface so easily and directly'.

Right Sara Robertson (UK), *Eating Her Words,* wall dish, monoprinted underglaze, slips and glaze, 29 cm x 23 cm (11.5" x 9").

Sara Robertson uses monoprinting as a direct way of transferring drawing to the clay surface. 'In spite of her innate facility with drawing on paper, Sara finds working with clay ultimately more satisfying ... at school she had read A Potter's Book *by Bernard Leach, and had resolved to become a thrower. However whenever she threw a pot she couldn't resist painting on it, and this was the start, 25 years ago, of her search for the right language to express herself' (from 'The Straight Path with 29 Curves', article by Rosamund Coady for* Ceramic Review*).*

Above Juliette Goddard (UK), *Woman,* Aberystwyth, 1997, lino cut print on plate, . Juliette Goddard, printmaker has explored the use of lino cuts and clay to produce very limited editions of plates, jugs or tiles.

Above Ivana Roberts (Croatia/UK), *Untitled,* Painting, monoprinting and drawing on high fire porcelain tile, 10 cm x 5 cm.

151

Above Rob Kessler (UK), *Le Déjeuner sur l'Herbe* (detail), bone china, onglaze screen prints.

From the exhibition Le Déjeuner sur l'Herbe, a group of works which explored the image of nature and its location within a contemporary context. It featured furniture, wall hangings and a series of unique bone china plates each decorated with a screen printed image of daises in the grass. 'Derived from a digitally manipulated photograph and printed in an unnatural array of different colourways the plates offer an abundance of choice. Each plate is divided equally into two halves, the one bearing the decoration and the other half plain white and undecorated, a format which reflects the continuing cultural preferences which straddle modernist purity and a post-modern mayhem, gluttony or abundance. Running in a single line around the gallery the plates formed an ornamental horizon, the format brutally contravening accepted notions of formal design, the stark contrast of the one half to the other, echoing the polarities of nature and artifice, shocking in its audacity, just as in Manet's painting' (Rob Kessler, 1998).

Left Kevin Petrie (UK), *Passing Clouds, Vista Bonita*, onglaze screen print on bone china (reduced solvent water-based ceramic transfer system), 1998, edition of 10.

Kevin Petrie is concerned with a controlled, reproductive drawn image. Silk screen transfer printing whilst less direct than monoprinting, has many advantages, both aesthetic and economic ... 'not least among these is the ability to reproduce artworks many times. This should not be underestimated by artists, for as the Italian designer and great exponent of transfer printing Piero Fornasetti said, 'Something which is beautiful does not become less so, even when it is reproduced twenty or thirty thousand times' (P. Mauries, 'Fornasetti – Designer of Dreams', Thames and Hudson, 1991, from AN, Jan 1998).

'I try to use the qualities of screenprinting as a creative and not just a reproductive process .... My pleasure in transfer printing derives from the qualities of surface which are unique to the processes. Only through onglaze transfer printing can the brightly coloured glossy imagery be achieved which, for me, provides 'gut reaction' pleasure. Bernard Leach, the father of studio pottery, said of transfer printing that, 'it is an invasion of the surface of pots'. While Herbert Read said that, 'the only real reason for decoration is to enhance form'. My work contradicts both comments and attempts to start to locate a new place for printed ceramics between the worlds of art, craft and industry' (Kevin Petrie, 1998).

The computer

A number of artists are using the computer as a tool for the development of the graphic image before applying it in various ways to the ceramic surface.

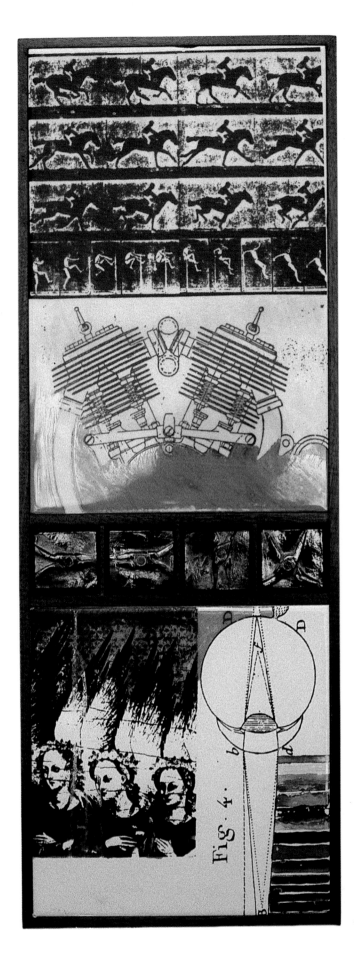

Left Paul Mason, *Before and After Muybridge I,* inglaze screen print decals on earthenware tiles, press moulded pieces, wooden framing 1997.

Mason's sources and influences lie outside the tradition of contemporary studio ceramics, there is no Leach, Rie or Coper here, but Paolozzi, Schwitters, Cornell and Ernst; however this work is essentially ceramic, for without the clay's ability to mimic, the kilns ability to fossilise and indelibly fix the print, it could not be.

Below Katie Bunnell (UK), *Bulldoglace 4,* sandblasted CAD/CAM design in porcelain, lustre and underglaze colour. 15 cm (6") dia. PhD research 1997.

Bunnell has been investigating the use of computer aided design, not only in three dimensions, but in its application to physically erode the surface of the fired porcelain. Bunnell uses both the front, and in this case the back, of ready made porcelain plates or saucers. 'This design is one of a series of saucers that embody ideas relating to gender and national identity. A drawing of a bulldog was manipulated using Computer Assisted Design (CAD) software into a lace pattern and used to create a ceramic surface through Computer Assisted Manufacture. The surface of the saucer, sandblasted through a number of resists and fired several times, combines low relief porcelain, lustre and under glaze colour to create a range of finished surfaces from one image' (Katie Bunnell, 1999).

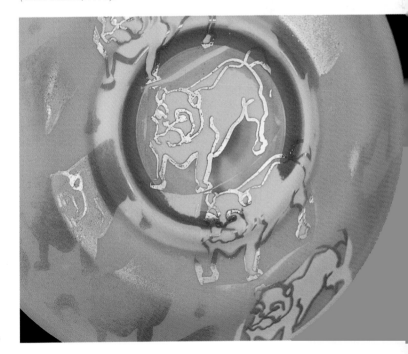

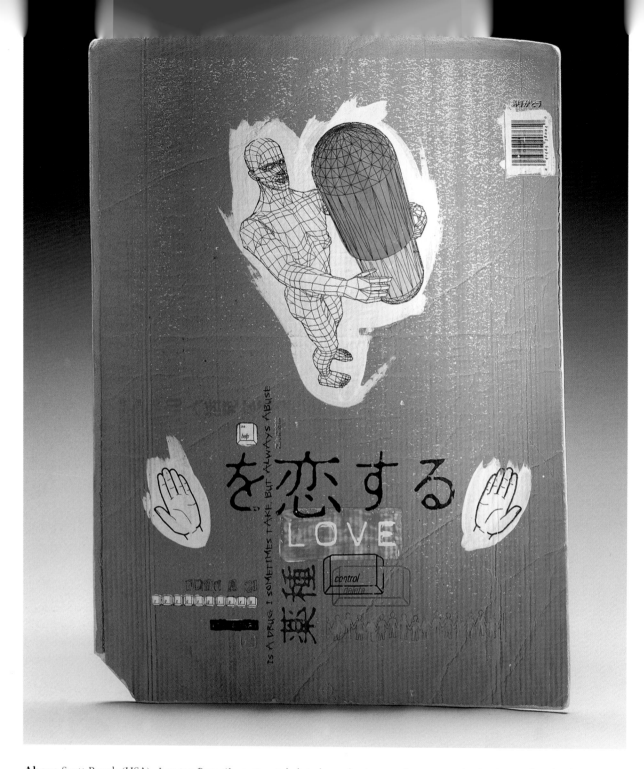

Above Scott Rench (USA), *Love is a Drug, (I sometimes take but always abuse)*, ceramic, screen print in glaze and underglaze on clay, 76 cm x 56 cm (30" x 22"), 1998. Photo Eric Smith.

Rench uses his computer skills to develop the complex imagery used in his ceramic prints. Unlike many painters and printmakers who have found the ceramics areas of colleges and universities liberating, Rench is one of many others who have found that they can be hostile environments to a purely graphic style of working.

'During several critiques of my work the comment was made that the pieces were all about imagery and didn't relate to the vessel. I got "beat up" about this for months.' His continued perseverance with the ceramic surface however has begun to reap benefits. Recent work is a reflection on lost love and his interest in Asian culture and its written language. 'I see the kanji as art objects first and its meaning second. I have chosen the card-board texture to symbolise the box I sometimes feel trapped in. It appears dirty and beaten up as it has travelled to many places and bares all the scars of its journey. Love is a Drug *speaks to my need to control, my loss of control and to say I'm sorry. I am torn by the extrovert who needs to express my feelings or emotions and the introvert who hides them.'*

154

Above Scott Rench (USA), *Destiny,* ceramic, screen print in glaze and underglaze on clay, 58 cm x 81 cm (23" x 32"), 1996. Photo Eric Smith.

Below Robert Dawson (UK), *Live Picture all the Way,* computer generated laser monoprint on earthenware tiles, 90 cm x 300 cm (36" x 108").

'I believe in using ceramics about ceramics (or painting about painting, or art about art) as a device. Through this I might be talking (visually) about the way I perceive things, the experience of the real world with its drifting perspectives, contradictions, paradoxes. I'm not interested in bluntly or crudely arguing some political or humanitarian point of great concern, or warning that war is a Bad Thing' (Robert Dawson from 'A Perspective on Tiles' in AN, June 1997).

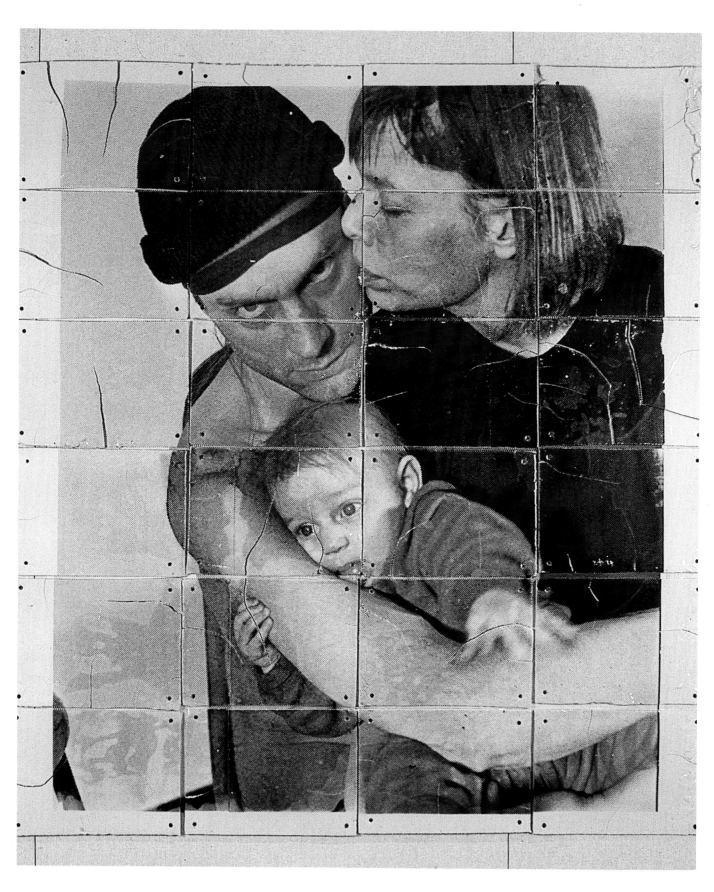

Above Peter Lenzo (USA), *Post nuclear Family Portrait*, photo
silkscreen low fire decal on porcelain, 153 cm x 127 cm (60" x 50").

Photography and the surface

Photography is an essential element in the preparation of the screenprinted examples of work, and also has a ceramic manifestation in its own right.

The first photographic image to be printed on a ceramic surface was produced by Lafon de Camarsac in France in 1854, using a gum bichromate system. By 1868 he was marketing a system producing fired portraits on porcelain, and today perhaps the best known adaptation of the technology is the long established use of ceramic photographs (of the deceased) on gravestones. In areas of France, Italy and Latin America they are a common sight in cemeteries.

Photographers like printmakers and potters can be obsessive in exploring new techniques and methodologies, and subsequently a range of photoceramic processes have been developed (with most fired photographs relying at some stage on gum bichromate). Like the ceramic printmaker who has yet to make any impact on the enclosed world of fine art printmaking, those using these techniques tend to operate at the edges of the contemporary ceramic, or photographic worlds, the critical framework of both disciplines seemingly unable to cope.

Right and below right Thomas Sipavicius (Lithuania/Hungary), *Who am I the Only One? 1–10,* 30 cm x 30 cm (12" x 12"). Porcelain with bichromate photographic print in oxides.

Sipavicius, working at the International Ceramic Studios in Hungary, has been exploring Victorian ceramic photo processes commonly used for tiles on gravestones.

Words and the surface

Words and clay have a long history and association (see *Glazed Expressions, Contemporary Ceramics and the Written Word*, catalogue for exhibition, Orleans House, Twickenham 1998). Ancient Babylonians and Assyrians inscribed and impressed writing into tablets of soft clay, oven baked or sundried. Later words have been used on mass produced souvenir and commemorative ware, and as conceptual art has relied heavily on documentation and text, and it is hardly surprising to find that this has also manifested itself in contemporary ceramics.

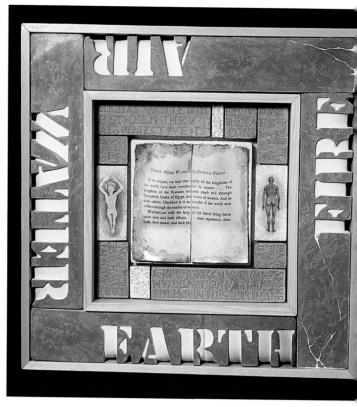

Right Linda McRae (USA), *Death of the Virgin, Manuscript Series From The Life of a Witch: The Sadness of Witches,* low fire glaze, oil on gold leaf, smoke-fired porcelain with photographic emulsion, 1994. The Two Texts: Hers (etched in the surrounding frame) from: *The Gynecologist,* Joan Lyons 1989. His (photo emulsion on book) from: *Malleus Malificarum* (the Hammer of Witches) Fathers Jakob Sprenger, Heinrich Kramer 1486.

Below Mary-Jo Bole (USA), *Detail from My First Dutch Lesson, Rust / Rest,* 1997–1999. Cast Silicon carbide refractory mosaic, cement. Bole uses glazed ceramic elements to create her mosaic images and words.

Above J. Opgenhaffen (Belgium), *Lost Paradise*, screen print on porcelain, 100 cm x 160 cm (39" x 63"), 1995, Medaglio d'Oro-49 Concorso Internationale della Ceramica d'Arte, Faenza (1).

The newspaper titles in this work have to do with drugs, accidents, the destruction of the environment, unemployment, racism, and corruption. 'Opgenhaffen uses newspapers and magazines — because of their contents, not because of their form — as formal points of departure and as elements in the construction of her reliefs. She looks for legible words in the always rotating newspaper tissue. Within the syntaxes of her relief construction, Opgenhaffen plays with the meaning of the words. Playing that semantic game, Opgenhaffen creates accents in a repetitive construction of folded texts, that are only legible in the rounded parts turned to the viewer. The parts that are turned away from the viewer cannot be read and consequently cannot be understood. Opgenhaffen's game of veiling and unveiling, legibility and illegibility, that-what-is-said and that-what-is-not-said is a comment on the press as well on the braggart discourse of the intelligentsia, and of course as well on the censorship that controls every form of speaking and every speaker' (Frans Boenders, (ed.) Art and Culture, pub. Musées Royaux des Beaux-Arts Brussels).

Above left Claire McLaughlin (UK), *Gloria,* earthenware, screen-print, 28 cm (11").

Above right Patrick King (UK/Switzerland), *Sarajevo 3.* Broken and reassembled plate, 55 cm (21.5") dia. Fragments are individually treated and fired (often separately) before reassembly, elements are printed over with text from newspapers, magazines, travel brochures etc. using a simple, manual, low-tech technique he has refined over the years.

'Intellectually, the work concerns itself with current (eternal) problems of society and attempts to produce pieces of art which aesthetically draw our attention but jolt us on closer examination into uncomfortable reflections about the human predicament. The unexpected setting in which the text fragments appear acts as an anchor in our memory for the political content. The pieces themselves express no direct political opinions, but are intended as chronicles of our time, much as ancient Greek vases or tapestries from the Middle Ages reveal to us the significant events affecting the past lives of the citizens. To counter the depressing, discouraging effect of the chosen themes, the reassembly and gluing together of the broken fragments into a more-or-less functioning object is a symbol of hope' (Patrick King, 1998).

Above Julie Eyers (UK), *Plate from the Wedding Service,* photographic silk screen transfer on bone china plate, 18 cm (7") dia., 1994. Text reads: 'No couple could be more attractive, him athletic like Apollo, her exquisite like Aphrodite.'

Eyers plays on the nostalgia and sentimentality of industrially produced commemorative ware, subverting it by using images of a (fictitious) traditional wedding, overlaid with quotes from mass produced romantic fiction.

Left Maria Geszler (Hungary), *Self Portrait with Cooling Towers*, porcelain window, silk screen print, 62 cm x 99 cm x 11 cm (24" x 39" x 4"), 1990.

'Writing – a multitude of signs. Writing – the V formation of a flock of birds, the particular drawings of foliage, our hands touching on doors, on latches, the mark of our feet in the earth. Trains write railway lines, the chimneys of factories breath smoke forms in the sky, the gardens whisper green humidity – I write my life in clay' (Maria Geszler, 1996).

The rounded painting and drawing

Above Jeff Irwin (USA), *Fallen Leaves*, earthenware, black underglaze, wax resist and sgraffito, 56 cm (22") dia.
Photo Jeff Irwin.

'As far back as I can remember I have drawn. My earliest influences came from cartoons and colouring books with their strong edge quality, black line and narrative story lines. My use of predominantly black and white was influenced by wood block prints I had seen in books and Chinese stone rubbings I saw whilst travelling in China.'

Above right Patrick Siler (USA), *A Great Head Looks at some Buildings.* 46 cm (18") dia. Thrown plate with painted vitreous slips.
Photo Paul Pak Lee.

Above Scott Jones (USA), *Ice Box,* low-fired white clay with painted coloured slips, 43 cm (17") dia., 1994. Photo Scott Jones.

Above Scott Jones (USA), *Oil Can,* low-fired white clay with painted coloured slips, 43 cm (17") dia., 1992. Photo Scott Jones.

Jones' interest in the appliances of the 1950s stems primarily from their design, their sleek lines and smooth edges lend themselves to his stylised, cartoon like renderings. 'The appliances Jones depicts stand like icons of a bygone era, having either already become or seemingly well on their way to being obsolete in an age of ever expanding technology and changing gender roles' (Sandy Cullen, in the Patriot News, Lancaster).

Left Stephen Bowers (Australia), dinner plates, underglaze painting (stencil reserves, brush work and marbleised background, 37 cm (14.5") dia. Photo Michael Kluvanek.

Bowers produces functional tableware, but with a highly decorative finish, which is the area he concentrates on. 'Most of my utility and tableware is made in a traditional "small industry" cooperative or collaborative way. I either design on paper or work out with a production thrower the forms to suit both utility and decoration.'

Above Stephen Bowers (Australia), wall pieces. Thrown frames, cast tile with underglaze painting and gold lustre, 33 cm (13") dia. Photo Michael Kluvanek.

The drawn and painted tile

Following on from Boyd, many choose to exploit the essentially 'ceramic' qualities of clay, slip, fired glaze and underglaze as their drawing or painterly medium . . .

Right David Alban (USA), *Untitled*, drawn clay and slip, 81 cm x 61 cm (32" x 24"). Photo Dan Meyers. '

I let the clay go leatherhard, and then carve, draw, and paint in a frenzy...
My reasoning for making such a heavy drawing is that I love to draw, and I
really love to fire. I spent time in grad school doing intaglio, and wood-block
printing... I was always excited by the blocks, and plates yet felt let down by
the printed image on the paper. The carving for me is what I am after. I am
able to address my need for clay, drawing, and printing on one piece.'

Left David Alban (USA), *Heart,* kiln shelf, slip, glaze, 56 cm x 30 cm (22" x 12"). Photo Dan Meyers.

164

Top right Herman Fogelin (Sweden), *Ikon,* painted slipglaze, sur-cru, 50 cm x 50 cm (20" x 20").

Right Denys James, (Canada), *Nadine,* terracotta and slips, 29 cm x 35 cm x 4 cm (11.5" x 14" x 1.5"), 1997. Photo Denys James.

A form of life drawing, James handbuilds his bas relief wall hangings working directly from observation of the model. He uses clay 'to express the subtle nuances of the human form and spirit'.

Right Renate Balda (Germany), painting with clay on paper and beeswax, 29 cm x 31 cm (11.5" x 12").

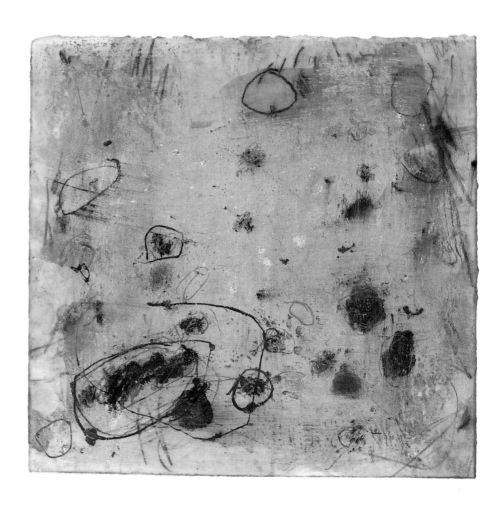

Below left Jim Melchert (USA), *George from the Life on Mars Series*, glazed kiln shelf, 51 cm x 51 cm x 2.5 cm (20" x 20" x 1"), 1997. Photo Lee Fatheree.

Jim Melchert has 'explored concepts that Bruce Nauman was defining in sculpture, Sol LeWitt in drawings, John Cage in music and Allan Kaprow in happenings. But Melchert's use of clay as well as other materials separates him from them. He may have started with an object of thought, but he has finished with an object of clay. By working in media that were outside the fine art arena, but by using concepts that were within, and by using clay in unexpected ways, Melchert has slipped in and out of categories' (Marsha Miró, in 'Jim Melchert: Mister In Between' in American Ceramics, *12/2). He also lays bare the challenge to those who would have us believe that ceramics always must be about form and volume.*

Below right Jim Melchert (USA), *Johana from the Life on Mars Series,* glazed kiln shelf, 51 cm x 51 cm (20" x 20 x 1"). 1997. Photo Lee Fatheree.

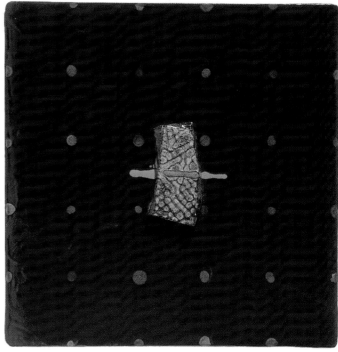

Above Thomas Orr (USA), *Three Suns in the House,* painted slips and glazes, 76 cm x 38 cm x 7 cm (30" x 15" x 3").

Below Thomas Orr (USA), *Suns with Shadows,* painted slips and glazes, 48 cm x 18 cm x 7 cm (19" x 7"x 3").

'Sometimes I feel like a painter trapped in a potter's body.' Orr attains his distinctive palette by layering glaze upon glaze, colour upon colour. They are painted over a white slip ground, and multi-fired, different materials and different temperatures giving particular qualities.

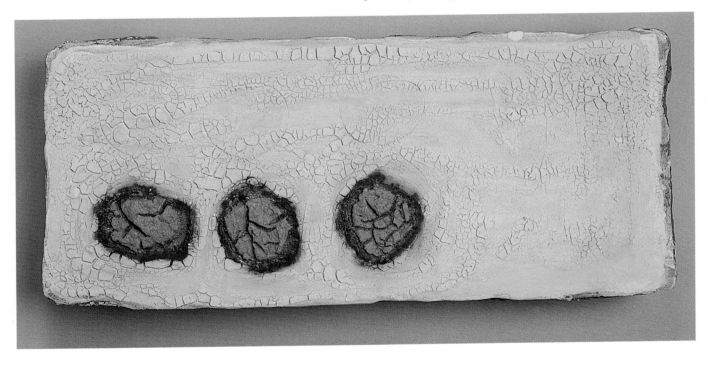

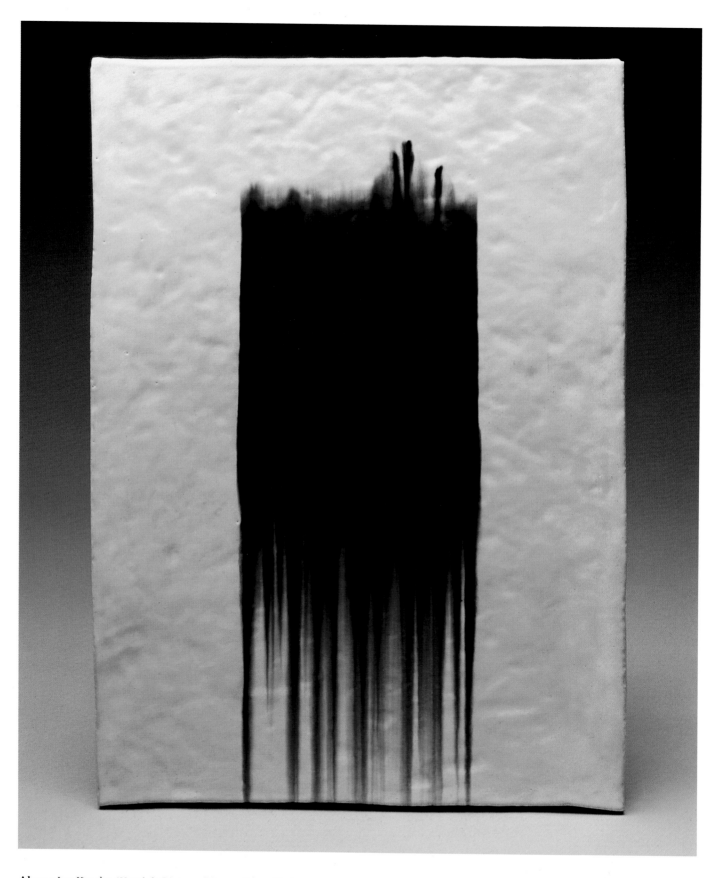

Above Jun Kaneko (*Untitled*) 54 cm x 72 cm x7 cm. Photo courtesy
European Ceramics Work Centre. 1996. Photo Takeshi Hatakeyama.

Durability and scale

Industrially produced ceramic tiles attract strangely uncritical collectors, numerous (dreadful) practical tile books concentrate on the 'how to do it', the decorative and the kitsch. Ceramic tiles have a bad name. But brick and tiled surfaces do provide an ultimately practical canvas, they have functionality, longevity and resilience. They are perfectly suited for artworks in public places. And they need not be tied by convention or tradition. In the 1980s Jim Melchert worked on large-scale tile wall reliefs, developing a colourful fluid glazing style that culminated in the production of a 220 ft long tiled wall. Others too have taken up the opportunities that the materials offer.

Right Lillemor Petersson (Sweden), *Columns,* detail sculpture, University, Göteborg, Sweden. Lillemor Peterson is well-known in Sweden for her sculptural brick work. In this piece individual bricks were drawn and marked in soft clay state.

Below Paul Scott, (UK), Main Entrance, Queen Elizabeth Hospital Gateshead, porcelain panels, painted underglaze and glaze, UK, 1994, 900 cm x 250 cm (355" x 100"). Commission for Gateshead MBC, Gateshead NHS Hospitals Trust, Northern Arts.

Above Ole Lislerud (Norway), *Partitur*, 1998. Main reception area of the Performing Arts Center in Ålesund, Norway. Porcelain slabs with drawings of contemporary music by Norweigan composer Arne Nordheim.

Right Paul Scott (UK), *The Scott Collection: Commission for Royal Victoria Infirmary, Newcastle. River panel* (detail), 180 cm x 65 cm (72" x 24"), painted underglaze on porcelain with screen printed inglaze decals, 1998. Photo Keith Paisley.

Above Paul Scott (UK), *The Scott Collection: Commission for Mottram St Andrew Village* (detail), 1999, 360 cm x 90 cm (144" x 36"). Painted underglaze on porcelain with screen printed inglaze, and onglaze open-stock decals, photocopy prints. Photo Andrew Morris.

'Tiles are too often square or rectangular. Scott's tiled pieces are like stained glass where individual pieces inform the overall design. From a distance the tile shapes and colours invoke a sense of movement and space, moving nearer, details begin to emerge until at close quarters, inspection reveals a wealth of painted and printed detail. In these slightly abstracted glazed paintings, print, paint, design and craft collide with startling effect. Some of the imagery and its means of presentation owe something to the products of pottery's industrial heritage, the fantasy landscapes of Spode's Italian Blue and Wedgwood's Woodland series, some to modern painting traditions and practice.'

Conclusion

'The use by ceramists of art-historical references may be the closest the modern artist can come to finding imagery that a number of people can understand, simply because art history and the museums industry are almost the new "religion" of our time' (Dr Jeannette Dekeukeleire).

'Avant-garde for the end of the twentieth century' (Greg Bell).

Today, 'studio ceramics' is a broad church, there are established markets, and there is academic interest and criticism. It is, however, still skewed to the applied or decorative arts. There are some in this book whilst making reference to ceramic traditions and practice are wrongly located here. The applied and decorative arts agenda with its fascination with objects, domesticity, function and form can be more open in taking into account this graphic work, but it cannot wholly embrace all of these people because the agenda cannot (philosophically) stretch far enough to do so.

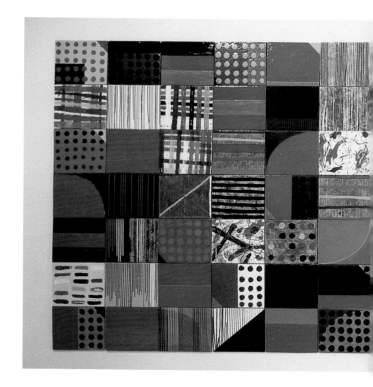

172

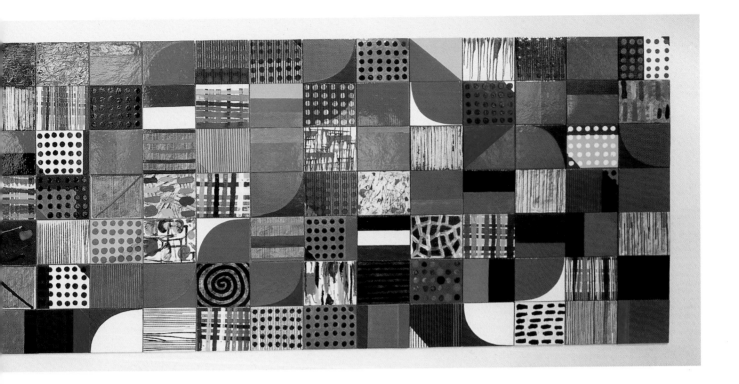

Some of today's artists working graphically in ceramics challenge the laziness that lumps and labels artists by the materials they use. Many chose to continue to work within the applied and decorative arts, widening its agenda, but others are aligning themselves more closely with other visual artists working in different media.

Some may feel that by grouping all these diverse works together, because of their material connections there is a danger of ghettoising the painted surface, much in the way that the Crafts in the UK have talked themselves into an obscure corner of the visual arts market. This is not my intention, nor I think, a likely outcome. The artists featured in this book come from very different backgrounds, movements and philosophies . . . but it is entirely appropriate that these works are considered in light of their historical (ceramic) contexts.

Artists have explained their differing motives in using the ceramic . . . and for many the simple reason is that ceramic materials and processes have unique qualities in providing an amazing material for drawing, an outstanding palette of glaze, colour and light unobtainable in other media. 'Ceramicness' is not just about form and volume, it is about fired colour and surface quality too. Just as pots need not have painted or graphic surface, graphic and painted clay need not always involve pots, or a three-dimensional object . . . ceramics can be about surface, a 'flat bed picture plane' too. The context in which image and surface are used together is an important signifier of that work's position in the visual arts market. Whatever the position the surface is much more important than has hitherto been acknowledged.

Above Jun Kaneko (USA), *Construction/Destruction*, 9.3 m x 2.6 m (30.5' x 8.5'). European Ceramics Workcentre, 1996. Photo Takashi Hatakeyama.

Below left Ole Lislerud (Norway), *Kansas City Portal Wall*, 1997, 12 m x 3.5 m (39.4' x 11.5'). Mixed media, basic structure of wood covered with porcelain tiles, glazes, phototransfer, silkscreen, decals and neon.

'The whole project is a commentary on the O.J. Simpson case and racism in general. Having grown up in South Africa I had an interesting background to make this commentary.' Ole Lislerud is another who, like Miró before, takes this 'unpopular medium' and uses it with vision and innovation on a large scale to remarkable effect.

Bibliography

About Types, Books and Prints, Didactic brochure for the Plantin-Moretus Museum and City Prints Gallery, Antwerp.

American Ceramics, the Collection of the Everson Museum of Art, Rizzoli International Publications Inc., 1989.

Anreeva, Lydia, *Art into Production, Soviet Textiles, Fashion and Ceramics 1917–1935,* Crafts Council, Ministry of Culture USSR, 1984.

Arthur Boyd, Retrospective, Art Gallery, New South Wales, 1994.

The Arts of Islam, Arts Council, 1976.

Bloom, Jonathan and Sheila Blair, *Islamic Arts,* Phaidon, 1997.

Boardman, John, *Early Greek Vase Painting,* Thames and Hudson, 1998.

Burrell Collection, Harper Collins/Glasgow Museums, 1997.

Castel-Branco Pereira, Joao, *Portuguese Tiles from the National Museum of Azulejo, Lisbon,* Zwemmer/Instituo Portugues De Museus, 1995.

Cohen, Harris and Catherine, *Looking at European Ceramics, A Guide to Technical Terms,* John Paul Getty Museum/British Museum Press, 1993.

Copeland, Robert, *Spode's Willow Pattern and Other Designs After the Chinese,* Studio Vista, 1990.

Dated Dutch Delftware, Rijksmuseum, Antwerp.

Dormer, Peter, (ed.), *The Culture of Craft,* Manchester University Press, 1997.

Dormer, Peter, *The New Ceramics, Trends and Traditions,* Thames and Hudson, 1994.

Erben, Walter, *Miro,* Taschen, 1992.

Failing, Patricia, *Howard Kottler Face to Face,* University of Washington Press, 1995.

Falchi, Rodolfo, *Concise Guide to Majolica,* Grange Books, 1994.

Fischell, Rosalind, *Blue and White China, Origins/Western Influences,* Little Brown and Co., 1987.

Glazed Expressions, Contemporary Ceramics and the Written Word, catalogue for exhibtion, Orleans House, Twickenham, 1998.

Harrod, Tanya, *Alison Britton, Ceramics in Studio,* Bellew/Aberystwyth Arts Centre, 1990.

Houston, John, *The Abstract Vessel, Ceramics in Studio,* Bellew Publishing, 1991.

Jindra Vikova, Benice Spa Publishing, Prague, 1997.

Konstants, Z., *Baltars,* Maza Makslas Enciklopedija, Riga 1996.

Lobanov-Rostovsky, Nina, *Revolutionary Ceramics, Soviet Propaganda Ware, 1917–1927,* Laurence King, 1990.

Lucie-Smith, Edward, *Elizabeth Fritsch, Vessels from Another World, Metaphysical Pots in Painted Stoneware,* Bellew/Northern Centre for Contemporary Art, 1993.

McCready, Karen, *Art Deco and Modernist Ceramics,* Thames and Hudson, 1995.

Metthey En De Schilders, André, *Keramiek en Fauvism,* de Stichting Sint-Jan, Brugge.

Nicholson, Paul T., *Egyptian Faience and Glass,* Shire Publications, 1993.

Osborne, Robin, *Archaic and Classical Greek Art,* Thames and Hudson, 1998.

Painters Ceramics, Based on the Collection of Museum Het Kruithuis, Museum of Contemporary Ceramic Art, The Shigaraki Ceramic Cultural Park, 1997.

Picasso, Painter and Sculptor in Clay, Royal Academy of Arts, 1998.

Pinot de Villechenon, Marie-Noelle, *Sevres, Porcelain from the Sevres Museum 1740 to the Present Day,* Lund Humphries, 1997.

Polder, Casper & Tichelaar, Pieter Jan, *Fired Paintings, Freisian Ceramic Wall Plaques 1870–1930,* Primervera Pers, Netherlands, 1998.

Poole, Julia E., *Italian Maiolica and Incised Slipware in the Fitzwilliam Museum, Cambridge,* Cambridge University Press, 1995.

Porter, Venetia, *Islamic Tiles,* British Museum, 1995.

Ravilious and Wedgwood, Richard Dennis, 1995.

Russisches Porzellan, 1895–1935, Badische Landesmuseum Karlsruhe, 1991.

Sam Haile, Potter and Painter, Bellew/Cleveland County Council, 1993.

Sauret, Andre, (translated by Howard Brabyn) *Chagall Ceramics, Sculptures,* Monaco 1972

Scott, Paul and Bennett, Terry (eds), *Hot Off the Press,* Bellew/Tullie House, Carlisle Museum and Art Gallery, 1996.

Scott, Rosemary, *Percival David Foundation of Chinese Art, A Guide to the Collection.* Percival David Foundation of Chinese Art, School of Oriental and African Studies, University of London, 1989.

Stangos, Nikos (ed.), *Concepts of Modern Art, From Fauvism to Postmodernism,* Thames and Hudson, 1997.

Stokvis, Willemijn, *Everything of Value is Defenceless, Cobra en de Keramiek,* Museum Het Kruithuis.

Terra Sculptura, Terra Pictura, Museum Het Kruithuis, s'Hertogenbosch, 1992.

Timms, Peter, *Australia Studio Pottery and China Painting,* Oxford University Press, 1986.

The Unexpected, Artists' Ceramics of the Twentieth Century, Museum Het Kruithuis, s'Hertogenbosch, Harry N. Abrams Inc., 1998

Vallauris, Ceramiques de Peinters et de Sculpteurs, Musee de Ceramique et d'Art Moderne de Vallauris, 1995.

Van Lemmen, Hans, *Delftware Tiles,* Laurence King, 1997.

West, Shearer (ed.), *Guide to Art,* Bloomsbury, 1996.

Williams, Dyfri, *Greek Vases,* British Museum, 1985.

Wilson, Timothy, *Maiolica Italian Renaissance Ceramics in the Ashmolean Museum,* Ashmolean Museum/Christies, 1989.

Index